MY DISCOVERY OF THE WEST

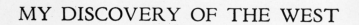

MY DISCOVERY
OF THE WEST

A Discussion of East and West in Canada

STEPHEN _{Butler}LEACOCK

B.A., PH.D., LL.D., LITT.D., D.C.L.

PROFESSOR EMERITUS, McGILL UNIVERSITY

BOSTON AND NEW YORK

HALE, CUSHMAN & FLINT

First printing, August 1937

PRINTED IN THE UNITED STATES OF AMERICA
BY THE POLYGRAPHIC COMPANY OF AMERICA, N.Y.

TABLE OF CONTENTS

PREFACE

MY CLAIM ON THE WEST: A PROPHECY THAT CAME TRUE

There is something inspiring in this building of a new country in which even the least of us has had some part. I can remember how my father went—from our Lake Simcoe farm—to the first Manitoba boom of over fifty years ago—before the railway. He had an idea that what the West needed was British energy and pluck. He came back broke in six months. Then Uncle Edward went; he had a gifted mind and used to quote to us that "the Star of the Empire glitters in the West." It didn't. He came back broke.

Then my brothers Dick and Jim went. Dick was in the Mounted Police and then worked in a saloon and came home broke. Jim got on fine but he played poker too well and had to leave terribly fast. Charlie and George and Teddy went— they all went but me. I was never free to go till now, but *I may start at any time.* Going West, to a Canadian, is like going after the Holy Grail to a knight of King Arthur. All Canadian families have had, like mine, their Western Odyssey.—*Stephen Leacock in the Book "Funny Pieces", 1936.*

CHAPTER ONE

MY PROPOSAL OF DISCOVERY

Why I left home—Travel Impressions and How
to Avoid Them—At the Head of the Lakes—
The City of Giants.

"Professor Stephen Leacock," said the chairman, every chairman, from Fort William to
Victoria,—"needs no introduction." Owing to
this bright thought, I never got any. So I must
introduce myself.

It has seemed to me that the East and the West
in Canada know all too little of each other, and
are drifting further and further apart. It occurred to me that if I went out and lectured to the
West, very likely the West would move closer to
the East.

I decided to follow the route of Alexander
Mackenzie, a Scotsman in the employ of the North
West Trading Company who made a discovery of
the West in 1793. Mackenzie went for pleasure.
He gave no lectures. I followed more or less on
his track.

Mackenzie made his way up the lakes to the
Kaministiquia River. I took the overland route
by the Canadian Pacific Railway, first as more
comfortable, secondly, as saving about a year.

I arrived at Fort William, on Lake Superior,
as the first stage of my lecture tour on November
25, 1936.

Whenever I go on a lecture trip to a new place

1

people ask me, "What are your impressions of our
city?" And I never have any. I don't seem able
to get them. All I can say is, "It seems all right;
I don't see anything the matter with it". A reporter asks: "What is your opinion of our public
buildings?" I answer, "They seem all right. Is
there anything wrong with them? Are they
falling down?" "How do our people strike you?"
"They haven't yet. Why should they? Is there
a riot on?"

In other words I've nothing but envy for the
regular travel experts who flash out impressions
like sparks from a flint. Put one of these down in
Fort William and he'd break out:

"Here at the head of Lake Superior with
Thunder Bay spread out before one, and the
Kaministiquia foaming at one's feet, one felt for
the first time the sense of the vast environment of
the Great North Land, an impression of bound-
lessness, as if here began the rule of boisterous
nature, defiant of man's puny power."

One might get that. But I didn't. I just saw
a big railway station, with red caps, and one said,
"Which are your bags?" and I said "These are."
There is nothing buoyant or defiant about that, is
there?

The travel-writer when he is done with boisterous nature, always turns to the personal element,
the psychology of travel. He breaks out with a
gush:

"The West is essentially hospitable. It takes
you at once to its heart!"

I didn't see anything of that. The young man at the desk of the hotel said, "We have a room reserved for you with a bath,—Is that right?" and I said, "That's right," and he said "Front 506!" That was all: the same reception I've had anywhere from Bangor, Maine to Memphis, Tennessee.

I have elsewhere in one of my books chronicled the standard way in which the travel impressions of foreigners are worked overtime in some such fashion as this:—

"I was met at the station (called in America the depot) by a member of the Municipal Council driving his own motor car. After giving me an excellent cigar, he proceeded to drive me about the town to various points of interest, including the municipal abattoir, where he gave me another excellent cigar, the Carnegie Public Library, the First National Bank (the courteous manager of which gave me an excellent cigar) and the Second Congregational Church, where I had the pleasure of meeting the pastor. The pastor, who appeared a man of breadth and culture, gave me another cigar."

But I didn't see anything of this at Fort William. A member of the city council said to me, "Would you like to look at our harbour?" And I said, "I will for a cigar!" And the pastor of one of the Churches asked, "Are you interested in Indian Relics," and I said "I am,—for a cigar." But somehow the formula didn't work.

After all what is there more dreary than being

driven round in a motor car, "seeing the town."
The trip carries with it a dialogue like this:—

"That's our Public Library."

"Is it?"

"I'll just drive round this corner and then you
can see it from the other side . . . . That's the other
side."

"Is it?"

"That's our new Court House."

"Is it?"

"The building next it is the Post Office."

"Is it?"

"But you can't see it very well from here, so
I'll drive round the block and then you'll see it.
. . . . Now you see it: that's the back side of the
Post Office."

"Is it?"

I don't mean to speak conceitedly. It's just as
bad, of course, for the man driving you as it is for
you. I know that, because again and again I have
had to drive a visitor round Montreal and show
him McGill University, and the Chateau de
Ramezay and the backside of the Stock Exchange,
and all the darn fool seemed able to say was, "Is
it?"

*   *   *   *   *

The point that I have been trying to make
above is that all travel-writing, and travel-
pictures in books are worn out and belong to a
past age. In these days such writing is quite impossible and I have no intention of putting any of
it into this book. It is no longer possible to tell

anybody anything new about anywhere. Since the moving pictures have come, everybody has seen everything. The travel writer's occupation is gone. A generation or two ago it was possible to write easy and endless "books of travel" with descriptions of towns and streets and hotels, like this:—

"Toronto is a charming city, albeit of a somewhat provincial type, laid out in a rectangular fashion on the northern shore of Lake Ontario. The principal thoroughfare, King Street, which traverses the city from west to east is 88 feet wide, while Yonge Street which traverses the city from north to south, is at right angles to it and is 88 feet, 6 inches wide. The Royal York hotel is a spacious structure containing 1,050 bedrooms, an abattoir, hot and cold water and all modern conveniences. The service is admirable and the cuisine is excellent. The courteous manager gave me a cigar. The typical Torontonian is about 5 feet, 9 inches high, with fairly wide shoulders and a dolichocephalic head with an ear on each side of it."

And after the travel-writer had written it up as Toronto, he had only to start it over again and call it Timbuctoo.

"Timbuctoo is laid out on a rectangular plan with no less than seven Presbyterian churches. Then Emir Wad El Foolzem gave me an excellent cigar, etc."

And so to sleep. If anybody would pay me to write that kind of stuff, I'd go all round the world

and never stop.   That kind of thing used to be
written up for Canada, long ago, by such people
as Mr. Buckingham, the temperance lecturer of the
middle forties; and is still written by women
travellers who take journeys through the Sahara
and come out on the other side, the natives having
refused to capture them.

There are still travellers who are simple enough
in their minds and enthusiastic enough over what
they see, to think it of interest to write, "We
steamed into Fort William at 10.15 p.m. and
pulled out again at 10.17".   Such people always
'steam in' and 'pull out': they identify themselves with the machinery. If they are feeling even
better, they 'blow in' and 'strike out'.   I didn't
'pull into' Fort William.   The porter did it for
me; and I didn't 'pull out'.   I slept there.

I knew that as soon as I arrived I would be
interviewed by the press, so I had the interview all
ready and merely handed it over.   It is far better
to write one's own interviews.   I took out a folded
paper and said to the reporter, "Here you will find
my impressions of Fort William.   It's a little dark
to read them in this light without spectacles but
you will note that Fort William impresses me as
having a population of 24,000 in 1931 and a
present estimate of 26,277.   Taken together with
Port Arthur, I should put its population at
48,777.   This is only my present estimate: I may
change it to-morrow.   The city impresses me also
as being situated on the Kaministiquia River at
the north western end of Lake Superior and as the

chief point of exodus for the wheat of the Canadian northwest. It thus impresses me as the chief port of the grain trade of the Great Lakes. It contains, I should say, at a guess, 10 schools, 3 firehalls and 13 parks. It looks to me as if the total value of the utilities was over $4,000,000 and I feel as if I were 960 feet above the level of the sea. I have all the more confidence in these impressions as I find they correspond very closely with those of Mr. Heaton as expressed in his Commercial Handbook."

All the same when I presently had a chance to get a real sight of Fort William I did get a very real impression of it. When I say Fort William I include with it the adjoining city of Port Arthur. They ought to be joined and called Fwather, or Port Arthliam. One can't keep saying both. But under any name it is quite literally what you would call a *gigantic* place. It is drawn upon a big scale, as if a great hand had seized a pencil and marked out in great bold strokes vast empty squares, and streets as wide as fields. So big is the city that they haven't had time to fill in the houses. Later on when they get time to put in lots of houses and buildings, it will be a fine city. At present it is all so spread out that a motor car looks lonely and a pedestrian like a solitary wanderer. There are great open spaces everywhere. Everything is planned to be a mile away from everything else.

All this is just right and in keeping with the surroundings. It was nature that suggested the gigantic idea. Outside, beyond the capes of Thunder Bay, stretches the great reach of Lake Superior. The bay itself would shelter a whole navy, and its towering rocky islands and shores make a navy look small and insignificant. In and through the town the sweeping circles and the branching mouths of the Kaministiquia River are quite properly all drawn on the same big scale. Behind the city mountains rise, quite close by, single and in chains, not like other mountains, soft and sloping, but torn and scarped and scarred, with upheaved layers of separate rocks that bear witness to millions of years of evolution. Geologists say that this is the oldest part of the world. I believe it. The Creator was trying out his hand: not in the dainty touches of finished art but in the broad, bold strokes of primitive design.

As with the town so with its commerce. For Fort William no gewgaws of retail trade in parcels and packets, no luxuries in little boxes. It deals in great raw primitive stuff, and it handles it not with hands but with cranes. High stacks of pulpwood rise as little mountains and keep sinking down as the pulp sticks go into the roaring mill, splash and tumble in foam, agonise in sulphur fumes, depart this life as living wood to come spinning out from great rollers, quiet and still, in their death shroud, as miles and miles of paper. Two hours sees it all through its death and resurrection. Wrapped in great bales too big to lift, machinery piles it up in cars, and rolls it into the Great Lakes steamers and away it goes down the lakes. Newsboys presently will be shouting over it in the great American cities. But in the beginning was Fort William.

With the paper goes iron and other ores; everything seems to go far away and to come from far away,——Ship-loads of sulphur from Yucatan for the death agony of the spruce sticks,——ship-loads of binder twine that was sisal in Honduras and will be turned into social credit in Alberta. But towering over it all, and dwarfing even the gigantic primitive industries are the grain elevators and the grain boats: the wheat that never ends, pounded and poured, spread out and sucked up, moving in a roar of machinery and a cloud of dust,——still and inert in the ship's silent hold, and thus all the way from the prairies to Liverpool. The elevators of the twin cities have a capacity of 92,000,000 bushels of wheat. But the figures don't matter. Make them as big as you like and they'd seem too small.

Yet for anybody who likes figures, prefers figures and can't get along without them, here are a few Fort William-Port Arthur statistics to write down. But don't try to remember them. In five years they'll all be out of date. The two cities have 30 grain elevators. They hold 92,000,000 bushels of grain. The combined city area has 340 miles of railway track in sidings. It has 22 miles of dock frontage. It can, and has, sorted out and unloaded 2,748 cars of grain in one day. It can roll out 865 tons of paper a day. It has behind it the water power of the Nipigon and the

Kaministiquia.   It has developed already over 100,000 hydro-electric horsepower, a statement which is more or less meaningless to untrained people like myself, but which gets a certain meaning by comparison.   It is using already about as much hydro-electric horse power as the whole of Nova Scotia, or as Alberta and Saskatchewan put together.   It sells it for 1 cent for a Kilowatt hour and lights its houses so cheaply and so brightly that you can play poker all night for the bare cost of the whiskey.

The scale of the emptiness and the openness of Fort William makes New York and London seem crowded, breathless anthills,—no place for *men*. I'd like to live there.   I'd like to go to Fort William young and live there fifty years till it had five hundred thousand inhabitants, and get old and half childish and prattle away about what it was like when it only had fifty thousand.

The reporter who received my "interview" seems indeed to have been pleased with it, for he added to it a very handsome tribute to my personal appearance.   "Professor Leacock," he said, "looks like anything rather than a professor."   This was high praise and he followed it with a flattering description of my physical appearance.   Alas!   I was soon to realize how greatly the strain and fatigue of public lecturing was to wear me down, as I could see by comparing the Fort William report with those that succeeded it.   The young man at Fort William wrote: "Stephen Leacock is a stockily-built man with a shock of iron-grey hair, a boisterous manner, an infectious laugh, and eyes that seem to be always smiling." Two weeks later, at Saskatoon, the paper said, "Dr. Leacock is a grave-looking man with a scholarly stoop, whose worn face lights up occasionally with a smile." More recently at Vancouver a reporter wrote:

"The little man, who is under-sized and practically bald, sank wearily into a chair, apologizing for his fatigue with a wan ghost of a smile." By the time I reached Victoria, the newspaper said,—"The poor little rat was found sitting in his golf bag, over the top of which his face peeped out with anxious solicitude. He appeared deeply dejected, asked for a glass of buttermilk and inquired the name of the town he was in."

I think I have got the last quotation right, if not word for word, that is the gist of it.

I addressed the assembled Canadian Clubs of Fort William and Port Arthur on the subject of our happy relations with the United States and what a pity it is that such happy relations couldn't be copied by the European nations. As a matter of fact there is no better instance of this than the existence of Fort William itself and its peculiar situation on the continent. It is what would be called in Europe the strategic centre of Canada. Whoever holds Fort William cuts Canada in two. Luckily for us we don't have to think in such terms. We talk of our cities in America as chief wheat centres, or principle hog centres or as first and second egg-eating centres but never as strategic centres. I hope we never do.

I had had occasion to realize this peculiar feature of the situation of the city during the only other previous visit I had paid to the town. It was in 1916. I had come there on behalf of the King of the Belgians being on an extended tour to give humorous lectures and send the money to the Belgian refugees gathered in the French city of Nantes. I went a long way. In fact the King of the Belgians had very generously said that he didn't care how far I went as long as I paid my own expenses. It was my first attempt to give humorous lectures. Till then I had only lectured on heavy political subjects. But this tour was intended to be a source of fun. I remember that my first lecture, at St. John, New Brunswick, was spoiled because the chairman announced it as "international law" and the audience believed him.

But I remember that in Fort William in 1916 the Mayor of the town, the late Sam Young, talked to me of how easily the Germans could have seized Fort William and cut Canada in two on August 4, 1914. It was even easier then than now. There were no aeroplanes and no bombs to reckon with. North of Fort William was practically nothing. A surprise party, prepared in advance could have landed from the other side of the Lakes, blown up culverts and bridges, put all the civil population, then only 30,000 on a couple of trains and sent them west, held the town and invited German reservists to make their way there.

I forget who won out, Mr. Young or the Germans. But it was a close thing between them.

The plan, if successful, would have blocked up all the Canadian grain,—there was no Panama, no Hudson Bay to take it,—and would have made all overseas contingents impossible till the town was retaken. This would have been a difficult thing to do, where nature had fortified it, east and west, with hundreds of miles of rock, muskeg and sunken gorges. So difficult indeed is the Lake Superior shore that there is one place where the railway had to be built in a three mile curve to get half a mile ahead.

At the time when Mr. Young explained the campaign to me the opportunity had long gone by. He was able therefore, without loss of patriotism, to throw himself with great vigour into the combat on both sides. Indeed it took him two years and cost him millions and millions to lick himself. Thus do generous minds often find a kind of pleasure in putting themselves in the other fellow's place and fighting on his side. Thus have I once had, thirty years ago, the privilege of listening to the famous Dr. Jameson explaining how the Boers could have licked the English by disregarding Ladysmith and Mafeking and making a rush for the sea. Thank Heaven the Germans never thought of these smart things till after they'd been licked. But the Fort William idea is at least curious,—and carries us back to the everlasting fact that any 'strategic' stuff as between the United States and Canada would mean destruction.   Our only form of defense against one another is to have absolutely none at all.   As to the Germans I don't think they are ever likely to start anything worse in Fort William than, "German Choral Society",—no, they couldn't.

And Fort William need only be interested in the 'strategy' of its economic development.   The grain trade and the Ocean Water Way, which is inevitably coming and coming soon, will turn it into a metropolis.   Add to this the Eldorado of Gold in the district above it,—in what was once Canada's fatal wilderness and is now Canada's greatest hope!   It is amazing what we have in Canada, the vast extent, the magnificence of the opportunity:—if only we don't tear it apart into nine pieces, one for each province to chew in its own corner of the den.

So I turn to speak of Fort William and the Waterway, and the great voyage from the sea.

CHAPTER TWO

FORT WILLIAM AND THE WATERWAY

The Dangerous Voyage of Fort William—Its
Contrasts of Sun and Storm—Of Dream and
Danger—The Great Waterways Project—
Bound to Come—Cheaper than Paying Relief.

By giving lectures in Fort William and elsewhere in 1916, I was able to send quite a sum of
money to help maintain the Belgian refugees
quartered in the French city of Nantes. The
mayor of the town wrote me a letter of thanks. I
don't know where he got his geographical information from. No doubt he was as vague in
his ideas on geography as all Frenchmen are: their
own country is so marvellous that they never
bother with others. No doubt also the mayor
used an atlas of the days of Louis XIV. He wrote,
"We observe with admiration that you have
penetrated even into the 'Country of the Savages'
and have made *the dangerous voyage to Fort
William.*"

I often repeated the phrase as a joke but the
more you think of it the more it seems justified.
It was, and it is dangerous,—dangerous in the old
days, and dangerous, for those who go down to
the sea in ships, even today. The first white people
who ever came to the mouth of the Kaministiquia
took months, even years to get there, months of
dangerous travel by river and portage and path-
way, often wintering as they went, with danger
on either hand; danger from man or from nature.

15

Many who went there, as the Irish would say, never got there.

The French in New France had from the first heard from the Indians of the great waters to the west, and that further on beyond was a great northern salt sea. Many had tried to reach it. Champlain, in search of it, got part of the way up the Ottawa.

Certain voyageurs,—nameless and without record,—went into the wilderness and returned with great loads of furs. Many never came back. All the country now called Ontario was overrun, in the seventeenth century, with bands of conquering Iroquois, killing and burning any fugitives that could be found.

Through this country at this time,—the year was 1658, went the great explorer Radisson as fierce as any Indian, and braver. With him was his brother-in-law, Groseillers, twenty-nine Frenchmen and some Indians. Their idea was to make the "dangerous voyage of Fort William." They left Montreal in June of 1658. They went up the Ottawa, and by Lake Nipissing, the French River, into and around Lake Huron. On Manitoulin Island they fought a war-party of Iroquois, and carried away eight of them, of whom three were dead. They ate the dead ones and burned the others over a slow fire. That sounds pretty dangerous travelling, for somebody.

Objection was taken to this statement, when first I made it, on the ground that it implies that the Indians were cannibals. So they were, to a great extent, especially the Indians of Central Canada, our own crowd.   The Senecas took the lead. They and the Ottawas and the Pottawottamies, were especially keen on eating the hearts of their enemies as a way of acquiring courage.

One is reminded of Mark Twain's grotesque fancy called *Cannibalism in the Cars,* in which a group of travelling congressmen, snowbound and starving, fall to eating one another after proper legislative voting as between majority and minority.   "The next morning," says the narrator, "we had Morgan of Alabama for breakfast, one of the finest men I ever sat down to."   A Seneca Indian would have read that passage with matter-of-fact approval.   The Senecas lived round where now are Buffalo and Rochester.   Their name is the same as Genesee and Genosha.   A great many hotels, restaurants and even lunch-wagons are named after them.   It seems quite right.

Whether Radisson joined in the feast indicated above, is left ambiguous in the original text of his journal.   He may have.   He was a terrific character, lived with the Indians as an Indian and joined in their torture of their enemies.   There is a fine account of him, from material out of the Hudson's Bay Company's archives, in Douglas Mackay's new and fascinating book, *The Honorable Company.*

Radisson's party wintered on Green Bay (off Lake Michigan) and there the Crees told them the way to take to reach the great salt sea of the north. They went through the Sault into Lake Superior.

From Chemaugemon Bay they explored a lot of
the water shed between the Mississippi and the
Great Lakes. They wintered on Lake Superior.
Next Summer they started for home, fighting the
Iroquois as they went (on one occasion five
hundred at a time), and reached Montreal in
August of 1660. The journey had taken two
years and two months. Their lives were at no
time worth two weeks purchase. No insurance
company would have touched them.

Yet they helped to make the history of the
world. Radisson had learned of the 'great salt
sea', the Hudson Bay,—of the fur territory all
around it, and how to reach it from Lake Superior.
He may still have thought, as Champlain certainly did, that this great salt sea led round the corner
to 'Cathay'. He ought not to have thought this,
because by this time English exploring ships, looking for the north west passage had practically
circumnavigated the Bay. But he certainly had
an idea of the great wealth offered in furs. He
resented the attempt of the French Governor of
Canada to make him pledge half his furs in advance. So when he went he went without official
leave, passed from Lake Superior through the fur
country and reached the Bay. Quarreling again
with the Governor, Radisson turned to England.
King Charles and his marvellous cousin Prince
Rupert,—the patron saint of our North West,—
itself once Rupertsland,—knew a good thing when
they saw it. The result was the Hudson's Bay
Company, the British occupation of the North

West, and my lecture tour. All this resulted from Radisson's first achievement of the dangerous voyage of Fort William!

After him come others, priests and explorers, scattered through the remaining century of the French Regime in Canada; Father Menard, who never came back, though his breviary and cassock were found years later; Father Allouez: and Marquette and Joliet and Hennepin. But French discovery drifted chiefly over the divide towards the Mississippi. The names of these explorers stand in their hall of fame, written up side by side as the names of the streets of Minneapolis with the red and green lights of the over crowded traffic to remind them of the result of their labours. But one, the famous Duluth, belongs also and very much to Fort William. He set up his chief post on the Kaministiquia, exactly at the site of the town. Then he traded as far as the Lake of the Woods and Lake Nipigon.

But as long as the English held the Bay and the French the St. Lawrence, neither one nor the other could make use of the natural and proper route to the fur country. When the cession of Canada gave the English both the Bay and the Lakes the "dangerous voyage of Fort William" came into its own. The new Northwest Company, organized from Montreal tapped the Hudson Bay territory from the basis of the lakes. Every Canadian has read of the grand old days of the company, with its fleet of canoes coming and going and its wintering partners. The farewell dinners, Scottish model, at Beaver Hall, took the place of the masses held on the French model at St. Anne's by the departing *coureurs des bois*. The members of both nations, on such a dangerous journey, prepared themselves to die, but each in their own way.

The two fur companies joined. The steamboat came, replacing the canoe for the lake journey. Then the railway took over the first part of it, and the 'voyage' was from Collingwood to Fort William. Thus went Lord Wolesley with steamers and a flock of boats, built in Collingwood, to suppress the Red River rising, that vanished at his approach. Young Prince Arthur of Connaught who was in the expedition has left his name in Port Arthur.

After that, the route was and remained by rail and steamer to Fort William with half a dozen Ontario points of departure, Owen Sound leading. Beyond Fort William the route after 1870 was a mixture of canoe and portage and steamer, as it was when the young Reverend Mr. Grant, later Principal Grant, passed through in 1872, from Prince Arthur's Landing to Fort Garry, on a voyage of discovery, under Mr. Sandford Fleming, to find the best way through the Rocky Mountains. Later the route was by rail to the Red River and down the river by steamer, till the completion of the C.P.R. hooked it all up from Fort William to the Pacific.

At first sight all the 'danger' seems out of it. But that is *only* on first sight. The water journey from Montreal to Fort William,—soon to turn into the great waterway from the sea to the West,—is among the most strange and romantic voyages in the world.   At one end, at one time of the year, it looks like the voyage of a dream: at the other, in the closing of the season, it looks like a grim tragedy of men against the sea.

In the Soulanges Canal, as the motor cars pass along the straight highway that borders it, is a great lake freighter moving up stream.   From the motor car that overtakes and passes it, it seems motionless —a little ruffle of foam at the bow and a little churning of the water about the propeller at the stern: no sound: no one in sight; the ship of a dream.   A sailor of the deep sea would scoff at the sight of it, the long whale-back body, battened down and flat, the high superstructure in front with a single funnel far astern.

There is no voyage on all the seven seas more romantic in its contrast than the voyage of the lake freighter, through the canals and up the rivers and over the lakes all the way from Montreal to Fort William: contrasts of sunshine and shadow, of still life and storm, of dream and danger.   In its passage up the long canal, the great freighter, seen from the hurrying car that passes it, seems to have fallen asleep, motionless: beyond the canals the river moves in a broad flood, the shores and islands intermingle; the United States intertwined and indistinguishable in the mass of foliage that crowns the indentations of the river.   Even the rapids, here and there seen, in glimpses, out beyond the embankment of the canal, merge into still life, the broad patches of broken water looking like great white flowers bursting harmless into blossom.   Out upon the lake, the water lies so still and clear in the light mists of morning sunshine, that the dream is unbroken still.   Well might anybody think that such a halcyon passage is but mere summer idleness beside the dangers of the open sea.

But now contrast the picture of haze and idleness, this motion that has fallen asleep, this voyage of a dream with the other end of the journey, the voyage down Lake Superior when the last of the great lake freighters, grain-loaded and battened down, puts out from the shelter of Thunder Bay, for its voyage down to Montreal.

And this time let us view it not as seen from a summer motor car beside the canal, but as seen from the windows of an iron-bound train circling the gorges of the Lake Superior wilderness.   Why *iron-bound*? because there is no other way to convey what is meant,—the scene easier to recall to the memory of those who have once seen it than to convey in words to those who never have.   It is the end of November: a sudden onrush of cold from the North West has precipitated winter. Mile after mile travels the train in warmth and light and human converse and comfort.   The bright luxury of the dining car contrasts with the whirling snow that beats in vain at its windows. Outside is rock and gorge, and mile after mile, hour after hour, the spruce forest that never ends. It is only late-November but the pointed trees are already topped and heavy with snow. Mile after mile, hour after hour, as the train winds through the gorges there is no change, no alteration: only the casual break offered by a railroad shed of the section hands. Here and there, nature as if in mockery imitates the semblance of habitation, snug outlines of hay fields and embowered meadows that prove to be nothing but torn openings in the hillsides; or here and there what in Europe might stand in the distance for some trim white abbey or chateau folded in green,——nothing in reality but a heap of great boulders buried in the snow among the spruces; or here and there again what seems like beacons, telegraphs and signals on the horizon of the hills and that are nothing but trees, frozen and broken to a mere 'lop stick' or single point. Of life nothing; the birds are gone: and over it all the clear cold sky dawning reluctant into the tardy day, and darkening into the early night. It is bitter cold. Passengers venturing a moment on the frozen platforms at Sudbury or Chapleau, return stamping and shivering to say that it is twenty below zero, feeling that their mimic adventure has deserved hot beef tea, or a hotter toddy in the observation car. Observation? Yes, just wait and look! The train has moved steadily all day till night is about to fall; and behold! seen a mile or two away is the open space of Lake Superior. Its waters are rimmed in great rock islands, rising grim on the darkening horizon. A great black cloud, heavy with snow joins the water in the sky. The dark night, as Virgil said, 'broods on the deep'.   The wind is rising as night comes, the snow drives harder at the window.   It is felt that there will be a great storm on the lake to-night.   Somewhere out there in the dark, just beyond the horizon are the great freighters, the last of the season.   All last night the winches clattered and the grain poured from the Fort William elevators and in the dark of the early morning their booming whistles echoed over the silent, frozen town to say good-bye.   They are the "last boats" out, heading outward through snow and storm to complete,—but sometimes not,—the last stage of the 'dangerous voyage of Fort William'.

It is this strange voyage,—now dream, now danger,—that it is proposed to expand upon a larger scale into the great project of an ocean route into the heart of North America.   On the face of it, nothing larger has ever been conceived in the transformation and enlargement at the hand of man of the pathways and waterways offered by nature.

*   *   *   *   *

The central idea is that of permitting ocean ships from all the world to come to dock at the lake ports, at Toronto, Buffalo, Chicago, Duluth and, preeminently for us Canadians,—at Fort William.   Is this itself just a dream, or a danger, or the opening of a new era?

The salient facts in the discussion of the ocean and lakes waterway are these.   The ocean, in the sense of salt water, dies away in the mouth of St. Lawrence somewhere near Quebec.

The salt sea ends, normally, at Murray Bay, the tides above Quebec at Three Rivers. Up to that point there is no question of draft or dredging. The ship channel from there to Montreal, by nature and dredging, is over thirty feet deep at low water. To make it seriously deeper would need lifting the bottom out of the river. But it doesn't need to be. The world's largest ships have a draft of about forty feet,—this is the Queen Mary class and there are only about ten of them. They need a dock twelve hundred feet long, special conditions of access and departure and other facilities. Only about four ports,—Southampton, Hamburg, Cherbourg, New York can conveniently take them. In other words they don't enter into the waterways problem at all. Ships of a draft of about twenty-seven feet, corresponding to the St. Lawrence navigation up to Montreal,—can and do carry the world's main trade in passengers and goods. There is no need to look further. But the present capacity for through traffic in the Canadian canals is limited to a water depth of fourteen feet.

The stretches of the one thousand mile waterway from Montreal to Fort William run as follows. First comes the Lachine Canal nine miles long, depth fourteen feet (five locks); then twenty-five miles across Lake St. Louis with no difficulty in getting a depth of twenty-seven feet: then comes the fourteen mile stretch of the Soulanges Canal (five locks); the deep water of Lake St. Francis, some thirty miles, the eleven

miles of the Cornwall canal followed by a mile
and a quarter of Farrans Canal, then some more
river, four miles of the Rapide Plat Canal, then
the final seven and a half miles of the Galops
Canal and then the open river to Lake Ontario.
These canals have a depth of fourteen to sixteen
feet and even less at low water. The full distance
from Montreal to Lake Ontario is two hundred
miles, one hundred and fifty of it river and fifty
canals. The open river and Lake Ontario give
unimpeded navigation for ships needing twenty-
seven feet. The Welland Canal connecting with
Lake Erie has a length of twenty-seven and one-
half miles and a depth of thirty feet. Across Lake
Erie and up the Detroit River, Lake St. Clair and
Lake Huron there is unimpeded navigation.

The Saulte Ste. Marie Canal is a mile and a third
long with a single lock and a depth of nineteen
feet. With that the ship enters Lake Superior and
can drink as deep as it likes for the four hundred
miles to Fort William. The total mileage of
canals to be passed is eighty miles; number of locks
forty-nine. The time taken by first class boats,
not unloading on the way, is about a week from
Montreal to Fort William.

It is difficult to classify and compare the ships
and tonnage on the present waterway. Some of
the ships are vessels that could be used on the
ocean: indeed a number of them actually come up
from the ocean to the lakes, but most of them by
reason of their construction could cross the ocean
but only with considerable risk: and a lot of the

boats specially made for grain, oil and ore, had
better not try to cross it at all.   The chief peculi-
arity of the cargo loads carried is, that, contrary to
physical nature, far more comes down than goes
up. The return for 1935 shows seven million tons
of upward freight and almost twelve million tons
downward.   In other words there is a chronic
shortage of freight one way.   The commodities
carried are overwhelmingly agricultural, this class
of freight being six million tons in a total of
eighteen million, as last reported, a fact reflecting
of course the export of Canadian wheat (four million tons) and as flour seven hundred thousand
tons.   Minerals stand next with six million tons
then manufactures four and one-half million and
forest products well over a million tons.

It is estimated that the Canadian share of the
cost of converting the waterway to one of a depth
of twenty-seven feet fit to carry real ocean ships
would be about two hundred million dollars.
This is the estimate given by the Canadian National Advisory Committee (1928-32).

The waterway is solely in Canadian water up
to Cornwall. All the rest is in water under joint
control of Canada and the United States.   Hence
the project is bottled up at the goodwill of Canada.
We can pull the cork. They can't. The United
States could find a new outlet across New York
state via the Erie Canal enlarged or some similar
route.   Such a canal is virtually out of the question.   Either the boats, ocean boats, must pass
under the bridges,—an enormously deep cutting,

or the bridges must open and shut, an impossibility across two hundred miles of farms.

In point of jurisdiction, the United States, (Treaty of 1871)), can use the River St. Lawrence as an outlet *for ever*. Canada could *abrogate* this. Anybody can abrogate anything, from his tailor bill to his religion. But Canada could only do it at the expense of turning our continent into an armed camp like Europe. Canada granted also the free use of the Canadian canals, but by negotiation not in the body of the treaty. Some authorities, even Dr. Oscar Skelton, Deputy Minister of External Affairs, say that this grant can be terminated. But I think perhaps we won't try.

It is to be noticed that I leave out altogether the question of power developments. I do so purposely. I don't think it need come in. The waterways project is complete without it. If we need the power we can use it. If not let it foam away to waste, as most of the world's water power does and always has. The power question is just a bye-product.

The only possible way to envisage the St. Lawrence Ocean waterway project is to look at it in a broad way,—to see it as a total first and to consider the final goal, not all the intermediate steps and difficulties. It is obvious that such a vast work would effect all kind of minor economic shifts and changes, all kinds of local and personal disturbances of existing vested interests. It is clear that to make so vast an omelette we must break a great many eggs.

Unfortunately nearly all discussions and opinions turn upon special interests, immediate effects or technical aspects. Naturally those who fear individual loss are more vociferous and more interested than the vast mass of the people who gain, it is true, but only in a diffused way and in the long run.

It has always been difficult to get the public to take long views of great national undertakings. When Thomas Jefferson bought 'Louisiana', (meaning about one-third of the United States) for $15,000,000 there was a loud outcry as to what on earth the nation could ever want with such vast emptiness. Alaska, bought by Mr. Secretary Seward for $7,200,000 was called "Seward's Icebox". The Panama Canal was only cut because the American government wanted it as a military asset and had to pretend to the public that it had economic value. Later on they found their pretence was reality. Canals and railroads were flouted in their infancy. The proposal to put a railroad all across Canada was ruled out of court as idiocy and bankruptcy. The old Mackenzie government of the 70's, as honest as it was timid, afraid to try to ride across the continent, proposed to crawl across, like a duck in and out of the water. While we waited for a transcontinental railroad, the United States built six.

There are certain fundamental economic factors that lie as the basis of the waterways proposal. Water transport is infinitely cheaper in terms of energy and consequently, apart from tolls and restrictions, cheaper in terms of money than land transport.   An engineering authority of the Great Lakes Paper Company told me that it cost less to carry a ton of sulphur for their mill by water from Yucatan to the Fort William dock than to haul it in a truck a few miles to the mill.   I think it was sulphur, he said, and I am pretty sure it was Yucatan: but even if it were brimstone from,— let us say Chicago,—the point is the same.   It is ever so much cheaper: try pulling a row boat over the grass and you'll see why.   As witness, look at the great and expanding commerce out of Vancouver via the Panama Canal, and even the commerce now beginning via the same canal to the Great Lakes.

It is a further economic factor that ships once loaded go on as far as they can go, like fish finding their way upstream.   Only when there is no more water will they hand over their load to a land carrier.   That is why, in the old South that was, every plantation on a river was a sort of sea-port; why Victoria, when Vancouver appeared, collapsed as a commercial maritime port, and why cargo boats from Liverpool go all the way to the Amazon till they reach Iquitos in Peru.   When they have to, vessels will tranship to vessels of another kind but only when they have to.

In some cases, lack of time compels ships to turn over their cargoes to railways as soon as and wherever they can.   Some cargoes are in a hurry. First class passengers, North Carolina strawberries and Japanese silk have got to move fast.

Otherwise they'll go to the bad or at least lose interest. But modern commerce is developing a lot of commodities that would rather move in slow majesty,—cement that will last a thousand years, oil that has already waited thousands,—all the heavy stuff that is remaking the transportation of the Ohio and the Mississippi, and replacing the palatial Mississippi steamer of Mark Twain's days, with its saloon load of gamblers and victims, by the oil barge moving as peacefully as a dead cigar. More than that, commerce even develops a type of cargo that would rather go slow than fast, just as passengers on a cruise consider not that time is money but that money means time. A better example is wheat,—ripe and ready before its market price is up: it has to be paid for somewhere; the longer the voyage, the cheaper the storage.

Commerce also more and more develops the use of vessels made for one thing, or specially for one,—oil boats, ore boats, coal boats. In the days of restricted trade few articles could form a whole cargo. Nearly everything was mixed freight,— and the air space left over, necessary to float the ship, was used for cattle and passengers. Such were the by-gone steamers of the old St. Lawrence trade, with the passengers on top, the cattle in front, the emigrants in the steerage, the cargo down below and the crew up in the rigging.

Now a huge plan like the waterways, seen in this light, is really only part of the remaking of modern transportation that is absolutely essential.

The railroads can haul the freight but can't pick it up: the truck can haul it but not far enough: the railway breaks (it can't help it) the passengers' finances and the motor car breaks their neck. Overhead flies the aeroplane, crows and crashes.

The railways, in our re-made world, will be rebuilt into long straight lines that cut through a two hundred foot hill and tunnel a two mile mountain; running with never a curve from one first class point to another: vomiting forth from its inside, when it stops, a flock of light trucks and swallowing in another,—as a snake does with its young. Such a train, a mile long and running at one hundred miles an hour can carry a wealth of freight. A stream-lined passenger train will carry its passengers, noiselessly and almost imperceptibly, at easily one hundred and twenty miles an hour on such a track,—and give them back their motor cars as a surprise at the end of it. The little bandy-legged passenger of the future, who never walks, with long arms like a chimpanzee and goggle eyes that see sideways, will step into his little car and off he goes down his local home boulevard, lined with linden trees, with only fifty miles to go.

*   *   *   *   *

One knows, of course, all the special arguments brought forward against the waterway,—that it would greatly injure Montreal and hence indirectly all Canada; that it would injure a host of existing freight carriers and routes and interests.

All these arguments seem to me to prove the case for the waterways, as a rubber ball bounces back from a wall. Arguments of just this kind were presented at the recent hearing at Albany in regard to the similar but smaller proposal to build a canal from the Hudson to Lake Champlain. They would only mean, it is true, that the new transport would be so obviously profitable to the community at large that existing transport would be wiped out. Just so did the stage coach wipe out the carrier's cart, and the railway wiped out the stage coach, and the radial railway wiped out the railway and the motor car truck started to wipe out both of them. The only case that could be made here would be for compensation of a private interest unfairly affected, where a relatively new investment was ruined by the new community enterprise. But that is only like giving a pension to the stage coach driver and putting the toll-gate keeper into an old man's home,—or asylum,— whichever he prefers. Those things don't touch the root of the matter.

But it is doubtful whether in the case of the waterways such argument is well found. Would Montreal be injured? The outgoing wheat would pass it by, except what came by rail, or could or would be diverted. The ships would come and go: the only profit lost would be that of storing, loading and unloading wheat. We have been trained to believe that that is very little. But Montreal will still have an enormous trade of its own, both out and in, as the distributing centre for Eastern Canada: it would still have a vast volume of transhipment of cargoes, because inevitably, for certain commodities, transhipment to special boats would be cheaper than the through voyage. And it would have a vastly increased opportunity for the development of all sorts of manufacturing industry, repair and outfit and building, stimulated by the waterway itself. If occasion were taken to make a part of the Island of Montreal a "free port," (manufacturing and building with tariff-free goods), it is quite possible that the waterway would create a tremendous "boom" in Montreal, and enable us to lift our crushing burden of debt, or even engage more aldermen at higher salaries.

It is argued that the waterway project is of no use because ocean boats are not lake boats and vice versa. One of the most interesting of the recent magazine articles on the subject contrasts the typical ocean boat with the typical lake boat. An average of ten modern upper-lake freighters shows a length of 535 feet to a beam of 58 feet and a draft of $27\frac{1}{2}$, along with 303 horse power. But the corresponding ocean freighter has a length of 427 feet to a beam of 55, and a draft of 32 and the horse power is 533. The lake freighters' hatches are in a continuous series on 24 feet centres, the ocean boat quite diversified. The lake boat is loaded and unloaded by gear on the dock, the ocean boat carries its own cargo gear. But the variation of draft surely only reflects the draft of the present Welland Canal and surely all this only

means that unified traffic will change the type of
boat, that terminal facilities for loading and unloading will also be unified.   To argue from the
plant existing now as if nature made it so for
ever, is like arguing the impossibility of a modern
railway from the existing fact of a narrow guage
line, with a wood burning engine and hand brakes.
Take a big wide look and it all alters.   All that
we know is that, on the whole, boats of fourteen
feet draft are not suitable for both services.   But a
boat of twenty-five foot draft is purely another
matter.   And we have to remember that in discussing the project in a large way we are to think
not of the boats afloat now but of the boats to be
built then.   Ocean boats, it is said, cost more per
ton than lake boats: but the new type of boat
may, as it were, split the difference.   The extra
cost per ton may still be economical by the saving
of transhipment.

One turns to the question of cost; if our share
of the waterway costs $200,000,000 and carries
an annual interest charge of $7,000,000 where,
it is asked do we get the money?   The answer is,
we have it now.   In the years 1930-35 the Dominion of Canada, as apart from provinces and
municipalities, spent $183,000,000 on the relief
of idle men and loaned to the provinces for
similar purposes $97,000,000.   It is better to
spend the money on new canals than to pay unemployed men to sit and fish in the old ones.   If
there is anything in the old economics, it is that
money *wisely and properly* spent on public de-

velopment, must in the end bring a return: and if there is anything in the new economics it is that the secret of economic activity is to 'start something', so that the coagulated wealth of the rich, clotted into the ore, called invesement, is smashed into the small coin of 'purchasing power' in the hands of the many.   In the old days of Barnum's circus a man in front of the tent used to shout 'Roll up, tumble up, if you can't get up any other way, throw your money up'. We need that man back.

The only trouble for us Canadians lies in the words "honestly and properly".   We no sooner see government money in sight than we line up in sections, with local interest everywhere clamorous. Worse than that, if one may say it very gently, in dealing with government money we are individually not just quite exactly what you'd call honest, In our private lives we are straight as a string.   We wouldn't cheat a bar-tender out of a nickle.   We can sit down to a game of poker and never use more than four aces.   We woudn't give a lead quarter to a taxi-man.   But let us deal with the Government, and this is different.   We have somehow grown up with the idea that the Government is there to be cheated, that, of course, it must pay too much, get too little, expropriate high and sell low.

So when we *do* begin to build the waterway, let us open the first canal with prayer.

CHAPTER THREE

SO THIS IS WINNIPEG

Winnipeg a World City—The Winnipeg that Was—The First Manitoba Boom—Fool's Paradise or Golden Age?—What About the Next Boom?

The visitor to the West,—the kind of visitor who writes up his visit,—is supposed, on his first morning in Winnipeg, to throw wide open his window and say, 'So this is Winnipeg'! I didn't. It was too cold. And there was no one to hear me except the waiter with the tea, and he knew that it was Winnipeg.

But I kept thinking it just the same. For Winnipeg in a sense means more to me, or at least goes back further in my recollections than it does even to most of the people who live in it. It carries me back to the days of the first Manitoba 'boom', and the recollections have with them all the colour and wonder of the first recollections of childhood.

*   *   *   *   *

"Winnipeg, the capital of Manitoba and chief city of Western Canada, situated at the junction of the Assiniboine and Red Rivers, 60 miles N. of the United States and 45 m. S. of Lake Winnipeg,"—so runs its eulogy in the most truthful of the encyclopedias. The Canadian census of 1931 adds, "pop., 218,000".

Winnipeg is one of the world's cities. Everybody everywhere who has heard of anywhere has

heard of it.   This is not because of its size.   Cities
of 218,000 are so common in the world that many
of them have never even heard of one another.
Winnipeg is a good deal smaller than Stoke, or
Dayton, or Stuttgart or Akron: Chin Kiang is
twice the size of it, and Bradford and Memphis
and Dallas and Mannheim all beat it easily.   In
the outside world, if it is not wicked to say so,
Winnipeg is far better known than Toronto.   Indeed I have always found that the only thing in
regard to Toronto which far-away people know
for certain is that McGill University is in it.   Now
the betting would be that practically everybody
in Bradford and Dallas knows where Winnipeg
is, but hardly anybody in Bradford knows where
Dallas is, and in that they've nothing on the
people in Dallas.

When then is Winnipeg a world-city, a city
known to all the world?

At first sight it seems a little hard to see why.
Its name only means "dirty water".   Its two
rivers lost all economic meaning years ago.   They
are only useful now to build bridges across.   As
to being 60 miles north of the United States, you
would say the same of Bowmanville, Ontario, and
who cares about that?

Worse than that.   Winnipeg is cold.   It is all
right to say that the place has a cosmopolitan
atmosphere,—I admit that it has,—but even a
cosmopolitan atmosphere needs a little steam heat.
Winnipeg has "six month's winter".   So at least
its warm admirer Vilhjalmur Stefansson admits in

his defence of its climate. The average temperature in January is,—I forget what,—dam cold, anyway. Even admitting that on bright winter days the thermometer often rises to zero, the place is cold.

Those who love Winnipeg,—and they all do,—explain that though it is cold it is "dry", and that being dry, you don't feel the cold. People always defend their home town in this way: London explains away its fog, Pittsburgh its smoke and Aberdeen its rain. It appears that the fog is not fog at all but *mist*, that the smoke is only *carbon*, and that the rain isn't really wet. So with that plea that Winnipeg is "dry". It may be, I saw no sign of it while I was there,—it seemed,—indoors anyway,—wetter than Aberdeen.

More than that,—the place is not only cold, it's drafty. It has the two widest streets of any capital city in the world.—Main Street and Portage Avenue,—but even they can't hold all the wind. With the thermometer at 30 below zero, and the wind behind him, a man walking on Main Street, Winnipeg, knows which side of him is which.

No; the only way to defend the climate of Winnipeg is to go the whole way with Vilhjalmur Stefannson and accept the doctrine the "colder the better". In that priceless book of his called *The Northward Course of Empire* he explains that mankind needs the cold, needs the stimulus of it and the energy that's in it. The languor of the tropics kills, the rigour of the north inspires and elevates. The progress of mankind is made by the cold, fights northward into the cold, using each new art of life and artifice of science to live further and further north.

It's a grand theory. Think of it next time you walk on Main or Portage with the January wind astern. Leave the tropics for the bums, the loafers and the poets,—let them have "a book of verses under a bough, a cup of wine and thou, singing beside them in the wilderness." But give me a tenderloin steak in a grill room on Main Street with a full-sized woman raised in the cattle country.

*   *   *   *   *

No,—Winnipeg is an all the world city, because its rise was part of the history of the world,—because its creation was one of the romances of the development of North America,—and because its fate,—its 'booms' and collapses, ardent hopes and bitter disillusionments, lie as it were close to the central mysteries of our economic life.

Winnipeg is a world city because the circumstances of its birth drew to it the eyes of all the world. It was like the sudden rise of San Francisco on the shores of the 'Southern Sea' or of Johannesburg on the unknown veldt of South Africa. It marked the invasion of mankind into a new and unoccupied territory. Till then 'Rupertsland' was one vast unknown emptiness. The stars circled in the Arctic sky over the snow that crackled at 40 below zero.   And then, in no time as it were, all was changed, and the Winnipeg that replaced Fort Garry was as widely and as suddenly known to all the world as the Johannesburg of ten years later.

This is why to many people who, like myself, had never seen it, Winnipeg has been a city of far-away memories, that carries in its name all the vividness, the poignancy and the meaning that goes with the memory of childhood.

I remember how the place was born, and those about me, the grown-up people of my family, had a part in its rising fortunes.

*   *   *   *   *

The 'boom' was of the years '80 and '81, and '82, but the great change began ten years before that with the taking over of the North West Territory as part of the Dominion of Canada, and the setting up of a little corner of it as a province. Till then Fort Garry was a fortified trading post of the Hudson's Bay Company at the junction of the Assiniboine and the Red Rivers.   'Winnipeg' was just a name locally given to a group of houses and trading stores scattered along the wagon-road beside the river where it met the portage track that led across the neck of land to the Assiniboine. Here lived the 'free-traders', men not connected with the company but trading and dealing on their own.

The creation of Manitoba made a shift in the whole scene,—like the "transformation scenes" of the theatre, so wonderful half a century ago.

The whole place, Fort Garry and all, went right-about-face, and looked south.   Till then, access had been from the north by the one ship a year that the Company sent through the Hudson's Straits: by this way came Lord Selkirk's colonists of 1811: by this way came, in 1842 to the service of the company, R. M. Ballantyne, the story writer whose books for a generation of English children were the only twilight that lit up the northern snow.

The route was over the ocean and through the straits and across the bay to Fort Churchill, up the river to Lake Winnipeg, then 45 miles up the Red River to Fort Garry.   Ballantyne took from the middle of May till the end of September to make the journey from Gravesend to Fort Garry.

Quicker access than that was needed now. Lord Wolesley's Expedition had helped to develop the route by Fort William and the Lake of the Woods. The rapid settlement of Minnesota offered a still easier approach.   The railway's had reached St. Paul in the middle 60's.   From there stage coaches ran, even in the 60's, three hundred miles across the Minnesota prairie to Georgetown, Minnesota, on the Red River.   They made the trip in five days,—fast going!   From there, as the crow flies, it was 250 miles to Fort Garry: but the little Red River steamer, "The Pioneer", was no crow: it followed the river and made it 500 miles and took 8 days to it.   From railhead to Fort Garry was a fortnight's trip, but you had to wait for the steamer, from one day to three weeks according to circumstances.

As soon as the province was established, every-thing moved with a rush. There was created a sort of economic vacuum and the air, an inblowing of men and goods, came rushing in. To begin with, settlement was pouring into the Minnesota district. It was beginning to be known in the outside world that the alluvial soil of the Red River district was even richer than Minnesota. Lord Wolseley's expedition had left behind it a regiment of British soldiers and after that had gone, there remained an 'Ontario Battalion' for which supplies must be brought in. There was the government to be housed, buildings to be made and new settlers to be provided for.

So here was Winnipeg,—a little place of 250 people in 1870,—with its hands full and its beds overfull and its saloons more than overfull,— hammering away night and day to make houses, and clamouring for lumber and transport—and traders and adventurers and behind them, slowly gathering to a head, the rising wave of real set-tlers. . . . The economic vacuum kept the little place at high pressure. Lumber that was worth seven dollars a thousand feet in Ontario sold for seventy dollars, coal oil, worth fifty cents a gal-lon 'back east', sold for five dollars 'out west'. No wonder the freighters could charge four dollars a hundred pounds for the Red River trip alone It was,—in the 'economic' sense,—'worth' it.

That meant, if you analyze it out economically, that there was lots of money in Winnipeg to buy things and few things to buy; that there was the 'money' sent for the soldiers and the money for the government and the private money of the new traders and store-builders and merchants; and this means, after complete analysis of what we call 'money' and 'credit' that there were a lot of people in Winnipeg who had a 'claim' on the goods and services of the East and could say 'send me this and send me that': and the only trouble was to find the transport, the way to get it there.

Then came the intensification of economic activity called a 'boom'. And the whole thing was sound, absolutely. No wind, no bubble about it; just solid economic fact, that can be repeated over and over again,—on the Peace River, in British Columbia, on Vancouver Island, in Northern Ontario, more or less all over Canada, wherever undeveloped resources, labour, capital and directing brains all come together. We have never understood the nature of a 'boom'. We look at it as a sort of economic fever. Not at all; a 'boom' is a burst of economic health.

*   *   *   *   *

No wonder things move fast in such a world,— where everything was young, everything to be done, and where everybody could make money out of everybody else,—nothing needed but transport, more transport, and more goods. These were the days when the railroad came into its own,—when people laughed and shouted and danced at the sight of the first train and loaded it with flowers, with the bell ringing and with merry girls riding on the cow-catcher! Alas, how dif-

ferent to the grim iron octopus of today, the huge
debt-carrier, the farmers imagined enemy! Something must be wrong somewhere.

Things moved! Especially all sorts of 'first
things'. The 'first' parliament met (1871) in
'Mr. A. G. Bannatyre's house', in the sitting
room,—three entire rooms being assigned to its
use, one upstairs and two down. The 'first
oysters' came to Winnipeg in February 1871. In
the same month came the 'first barber': but his
business, I am sure, was trimming beards, not re-
moving them: Winnipeg knew no such effeminacy
as a clean shave till many years later. With the
barber appeared shortly a 'first baker' and a 'first
harness maker'. It was like the days of Pharaoh.
Dr. C. J. Bird in the summer of 1871 set up the
'first soda water fountain': they had a whiskey
fountain already. More ominous still is the
chronicled record that on December 14, 1870, Mr.
Stewart Mulvey gave the 'first public lecture' in
Winnipeg. He chose as his topic, "True Great-
ness", and we are told that he was listened to
"with great pleasure". It's a cruel phrase to use of
any lecturer. Laughter, if you like, derision, anger,
excitement,—but not "great pleasure".

Music also sprang to life and woke to harmony.
We read in the charming volume on *Winnipeg's
Early Days*, written by my old friend, Mr. W. J.
Healy, the Provincial Librarian, that "the first
hand organ was played in Winnipeg in 1876".
Mr. Healy adds that it was the only one, then or
since, but does not say where the man was buried.

But the main thing in the morning of the life of Winnipeg was the initiation of public enterprises,—especially with a charter (from Mr. Bannatyre's sitting room) or, simpler still,—application for a charter. Each new idea was taken up with a hurrah! and if no money came in, they dropped as easily and no one cared. There was a "Bank of Rupertsland,"—hurrah!—and then another, the Bank of Manitoba! Neither of them happened. There was an application for a joint stock company for the construction of a railway "passing through the town of Winnipeg to connect with the nearest of the Minnesota railways"—; a "Bridge company", that never built bridges—a "General Manufacturing and Investment Co." that never went further and a "Manitoba Brewing Company" whose future was fully realized.

All this in the early days before the real 'boom' began. Measured statistically progress was slow. There were 250 people in Winnipeg in 1870, and 817 in St. Boniface and only 1,565 pure white people in all Manitoba. By 1872 the town still had only reached 1,467, but even in 1882, when all the world had heard of it, the population of Winnipeg was still only 7.900 and that of all Manitoba only a little over 60,000.

But the ground swell that indicated the tidal wave that was to come, appeared years before the boom in the high, the staggering prices paid for real estate while the place was still little more than a hamlet. In 1872 the Hudson's Bay Company,

so Grant tells us, sold as building lots thirteen
of their five hundred acres about Fort Garry and
received $7,000 an acre for them.

*   *   *   *   *

The real boom could not come in these early
years. The setting was not ready: but the course
of the next ten years prepared it. The 'railway'
reached Winnipeg, by way of St. Paul and Minnesota in 1878. The Homestead Act of 1875 and
the surveys that followed it opened up the North-
west for all the world. And the great depression
of the 70's that lay with increasing dead weight on
Europe, and impoverished the farmers of Ontario
set loose the great migration to the land of hope.

*   *   *   *   *

It is here that my own personal recollections, as
a boy of eleven years connect with the period. I
give them, not for any personal value, but as reflecting the men and things of the 'boom' period,
the circumstances that occasioned the migration
from older Canada to Manitoba, the ardent hopes
that went with it and the bitter disillusionment in
which it ended. To my mind the tragedy of the
'boom' is that it never should have collapsed.
Good old Colonel George Ham called it in his
memoirs a 'fool's paradise'. If so it was a paradise
lost. We must regain it.

*   *   *   *   *

We lived, and had lived, for five years before
the Manitoba migration, on a Canadian farm, four
miles back from Lake Simcoe, in an isolation not
known today, even in the Arctic. The nearest vil-

lage was four miles away, through great cedar swamps and over narrow roads,——a horse and buggy or a sleigh the only means of communication. There was no railway. Newspapers we never saw. No one came and went. There was nowhere to come and go. And the stillness of the winter nights was as silent as eternity.

Then came all about us the hard times brought about by the fall of all farm prices. Mortgages fell like great snowflakes on the farms. People were 'turned out' and 'sold up' and moved away or 'went to the States', or simpler still, died. And then all of the people began talking of the place we then called Manitobah,——and they used to ask "Does your father think of going to Manitobah?" They didn't know that the word meant 'God's country', but it sounded like that to them.

Just at that time there came to us from England my uncle, my father's youngest brother, E. P. Leacock, still dimly remembered in Winnipeg as an outstanding 'character' of the boom. He was an adventurous spirit, full of brains, and attraction; as visionary as Tartarin, as loud as Falstaff, bearded and jovial as a Plantagenet. Nothing would do him but my father must go with him to Manitoba. The "Star of Empire" he told us children, "glitters in the West". So it was to, for a little while.

*   *   *   *   *

So we had a 'sale' at our farm, as countless other Ontario people did. The whiskey for the sale cost more than the thin animals and broken

implements brought in.   But that didn't matter.
The star was glittering.   My uncle wiped out all
disappointment with a laugh and off they went.
We children stayed behind to follow later: though
as a family we never followed.   But my father
and uncle 'hit' Winnipeg just as the boom rose to
its height and my uncle, at least, rode on the very
crest of it, triumphant.

*   *   *   *   *

I have always felt that there must be something exhilarating, stimulating, superhuman in
the rushing, upward life of a boom town,—A San
Francisco of the 50's, a Carson city of the 60's, a
Winnipeg of the 80's.   The life of the individual
fits into the surroundings as into a glove—the
'world' no longer means something far away,
something in the papers,—It is right there.   In
the life of the great cities of today the individual
is crushed, lost, is nothing.   In the boom town his
life is life itself.   There everybody is somebody.
'Character' springs like a plant and individuality
blooms like a rose: and forthwith there are gay
people, brave people, and queer people,—room
for everybody to be something; not the crushed
dead-level uniformity of the metropolis.   Everybody becomes, as in Charles Dicken's America, 'a
remarkable man': indeed we all are, in reality, if
looked into deeply enough.

In such a setting politics swell into grandeur:
social life becomes a whirl—life itself a day-to-day
adventure, and the future an infinite vista.   So
was it with Winnipeg of the boom, as beside which

the New York and London of today are dull and commonplace.

*   *   *   *   *

My father and my uncle arrived in Winnipeg just as the boom was rising to its height. George Ham has described for us the frantic activity of speculation which went with, indeed sprang from, the economic basis of the opening-up of a new country,—

"Auction sales", he writes, "were held daily and nightly. Property changed hands quickly at greatly enhanced values. The craze spread to the rural districts. Surveyors and map artists worked overtime to fill orders. If ever there was a fool's paradise, it sure was located in Winnipeg. Men made fortunes—mostly on paper—and life was one continuous joy-ride."

But I am convinced that Colonel Ham, like so many others, has mistaken the mere surface for the foundation, the foam for the water. If there is room for 300,000 people in Winnipeg now, so there was then,—for a prairie population of nearly three million now, so there was then. No part of the world is full till mankind exploits and uses its uttermost resources. Leaving out of count the places,—London, Belgium and such,—where peo-ple live not on resources under their feet, but on resources carried in and out, the filling up of the world has happened so far in only a few crowded areas of India, China, Java and the like. Most of it is still relatively empty,—our country and Australia almost completely so.   Our only trouble is that we don't know how to begin.

But the outward and visible sign of the real meaning of the boom in Winnipeg in 1881 was that there was 'bread and work for all'; jobs for everybody, plain or skilled it didn't matter. Everybody was counted a skilled labourer till he blew himself up or broke his leg and proved that he wasn't. I recall that a young man who went out with my father and uncle, straight off an Ontario farm, got a job the first day running the engine in a steam laundry. He didn't know how to run it but that didn't matter. No one else did. He blew himself up the same day. That didn't matter either. I doubt if they even went to look for him.

My father opened a 'real-estate office' with a sign in blue and gold thirty feet long. He had with him an English partner, a Captain Desborough,—the type of those drawn from the old country by the magnet of Manitoba. The captain had been a 'public school' boy, still knew the first line of the first book of Virgil and commanded great respect with it in the saloons on Main Street. He and my father lasted nearly a year before they blew up.

My uncle had a larger career,—went up like a rocket; was in everything,—railway companies, land companies, and in the parliament of Manitoba. I remember how a group of them came down to Toronto a little later, (when I was a school-boy there),—along with John Norquay, the famous prime minister. I remember what huge men they seemed, all bearded like Assyrians and wearing the buffalo coats of the period! There are no such men now. That barber who first insinuated himself into Main Street, has got in his work.

*   *   *   *   *

So the boom broke: and after its collapse arose a foolish theory as if the mere buying and selling had anything to do with what happened. Buying and selling back and forward is as empty economically as a poker game. Collectively no one is richer or poorer. It was not because the buying and selling stopped that the boom broke, but because the hammerers stopped clattering on Main Street, our navvies stopped digging on the prairies. We 'called it a day' too soon.

This problem when the new boom begins we shall have to face again. The essential point for its solution will be to keep the economic, physical life of development of resources by work and capital running well ahead of its mere reflection in pecuniary values. There must be the substance or the shadow vanishes.

*   *   *   *   *

One last feature remains to record and to commend in the Winnipeg of the bye-gone days,— a feature that left upon it a mark that it still wears. This is the cosmopolitan, world-wide outlook of Winnipeg, that shows itself in the city press, in the public organisations and in the university and learned societies. The city runs true to its first form.   It was from its birth a cosmopolitan place, a meeting place of people from all over the world. It was born, so to speak, into the sunlight of the larger world, and had nothing of the long slow twilight of the growth of other cities.   George Grant, the later principal of Queen's, noticed this when he visited the place for the second time, in 1881.   "Winnipeg", he said, "is London or New York on a small scale.   You meet people from all over the world."   A result of this was the appearance in the little town of almost every known form of institution and patriotic society, a historical club, a St. Andrew's society, with another society for St. George and one for St. Patrick. The whole social life was buttressed, perhaps stimulated, with a supply of saloons that attracted the notice of every visitor.

Winnipeg, like the rest of us, was born in mingled sin and righteousness.   Purged now of its sin, it keeps the virtue of its cosmopolitan outlook.   Buried in the heart of a continent, it still looks over the rim of it in all directions.

CHAPTER FOUR

WINNIPEG AND THE EAST

Winnipeg the Economic Centre of the West—
Its Fate Dependent on East and West Re-
lations—The Case Against the East: The
Tariffs, the Debt, the Money Power.

It would not do to say that Winnipeg represents the brain centre of the North West. That
proposition would be warmly debated at Edmonton, and flatly denied at Moosejaw. But it can
be properly called the focus of the economic life
of the prairie provinces. Its whole fate and
circumstances depend on their welfare: and in
turn contribute to it. If therefore opportunity,
privilege and power are ill-balanced as between
the East and the West of Canada,—in other words
if the case against the East is justified,—it is
Winnipeg that feels the grievance first and most.
It is not like Vancouver. It cannot link up with
an outside world. It is not like a farm district in
British Columbia or on the Peace which, if it has
to, can chop its own wood and live off its garden
and barnyard. Winnipeg has no outlet but the
East, and no basis but the West. It is a sort of
economic funnel, or if that term is too dead and
mechanical, it is the main artery of the economic
life of the West.

The geographical situation of Winnipeg is
peculiar. It is reproduced by no other great city
in the world. Winnipeg is the only front door,—
geography makes it so,—to all the vast territory

of the North West.   Access by the back-door
(Vancouver) is taking on a new importance.
But as the front-door Winnipeg must remain.
There is no other way round.   Whether migration
and trade move by the Lakes or by rail, Winnipeg
is the way in.

This means that Winnipeg and all that it has
been and may be commercially, is based on the
prairie territory beyond it.   Prosperity in the
prairies means wealth and expansion for Winnipeg: depression out beyond puts Winnipeg in the
dark.

Hence all the grievances of the West focus on
Winnipeg.   All the ills of all the provinces and
all the parts of them press on Winnipeg.   It is
therefore in connection with the fate of Winnipeg
that one finds a common ground for setting together all this "Bill of grievances" now drawn up
by the people of the West against the so-called
"money power" of the East.   The West, that is
to say, has an idea that there is a thing in the East
called the "money power" which piles up money
in the East as the moon piles up the tides, and
leaves the West in low water with the dry shoals
sticking out.   The West has a further idea that the
"money power" has created an ingenious con-
trivance called the tariff from which the East gets
all the benefit and the West none; which compels
the farmer on the prairies to buy all the things he
needs for his work,—implements and tractors,—
or needs for his life,—motors, clothes, boots,
shoes, everything,—at high prices; while just

south of him across an imaginary line, another set
of farmers, situated otherwise just as he is, buy the
same things at much lower prices.   From this
promised land the Western farmer is shut out.

The West is overwhelmingly in debt,—public
and private, municipal and mortgage, house and
home.   It sits like a debtor in a prison, its heart
full of curses against the Eastern "money lender".
With the money lender goes a work of sin called a
bank, with the right to make all the money it
likes out of paper, the people's right stolen from
them.

With that, the drought, seven years of it, the
scourge of God, that the East can't, or won't
alleviate or at least properly allow for.   Such
grievences among less controlled, fiercer people
have before now put arms in their hands.   Let the
East take care !

So sits the West, scowling and muttering at the
East as it imagines it,—seeing nothing but plutocrats and money-lenders, unaware of the dark
shadow that has equally fallen over what were
once the sunlit towns of Ontario, unaware of the
crowded tenements and the hungry slums of Montreal, and of the feet that beat the pavement looking for a job.

And the East, itself tormented, looks back in
anger and sees nothing in the West but a pack of
Bolsheviks, Ukrainians, liars,—who don't keep
their bond and forget, or never had, the tradition
that made the British people.

There is where we are in Canada.   Hurry!
Hurry!   We must do something.

*   *   *   *   *

Take the grievances one by one, and first of all
the oldest and the simplest, the one that we always
have with us,—the tariff.

Let there be no misunderstanding.   I am not
arguing here either for free trade or for protection.
It is not here a question of that.   It is a question
of the hopeless misfit that either of them, without
adjustment, makes in our country, by reason of
the everwhelming predominance of manufacture
at one end, and agriculture at the other.   Free trade
would ruin half our Eastern cities: protection
half ruins all our Western farms.

Here are some of the official statistics that go to
show that in Canada manufacture centres are
overwhelmingly in the East.

Of the 24,000 Canadian manufacturing estab-
lishments, 17,000 are in Ontario and Quebec: of
the $5,500,000,000 returned as invested in manu-
facture, $4,000,000,000 is in the plants of
Ontario and Quebec: and of the people who get
their living from manufacture, in all 550,000
people and their dependents, 437,000 belong to
Ontario and Quebec.   The three prairie provinces
all put together have only 38,000 wage-earners in
factories.   But even that, being drawn from government statistics, understates, indeed misstates the
case.   The more one deals with government
statistics, the more one feels the need of improving
on them.   I remember once asking an electioneering

friend of mine, just after he had made a brilliant and convincing speech, whether he got his figures from the government statistics. "No," he said, "they're no good. I always make up my own."

Apply this to so-called "Western manufactures" and we find that the government classifies as such all the whole business of printing and distributing the local newspapers and puts in the "central electric stations" that generate electric power as manufactures. One might as well put in the barber with his shampoo or the man that turns the grindstone.

Take away these and with them the purely localized manufactures that spring from agriculture itself,—the flour mills and the packing plants and the local sawmills, and what have you got? Just about nothing.

Turn to the imposing list that makes up in our Canadian classification the "forty leading industries"; it is a pity they chose forty, it sounds too much like Ali-Baba. Here we find the automobile industry with a wages and salaries pay list of 8,000 people: the metal industries (smelting, casting, forging, iron and steel, etc.) with 23,000; electrical industries, not generating power, but manufacturing goods, 11,000; the textile and clothing industries, 31,000; add to that such vast industries as pulp and paper (24,000), tobacco making (8,000), boots and shoes (14,000), and you get a grand total of 377,000 "souls",—if they haven't lost them under protection.

Now turn these things into terms of "con-

sumption goods" that the Westerner uses,—the
clothes on his back, the clothes off his wife's, the
motor car that is in his garage (or isn't), his
children's boots and shoes (if they're not bare-
foot), the artificial silk stockings of his grown-up
daughters,—see what a bill of indictment, what
a flood of sentiment can be worked up over it!

On all these things the farmer, to import them,
pays a duty, or pays a higher price, or goes without them: his motor car, 17½ per cent.; on his
linen shirt, 25 per cent., and three cents a lb. on
his celluloid shirt bosom, (if he tries to escape that
way), 15 per cent.; on his paper dickey (a low
subterfuge), 22½ per cent.; on his "shorts",—
for playing Badminton, 15 per cent., and so on,
right down to his shoe laces.

I am not denying that the Western farmer has
his "free list": though I doubt if he draws much
comfort from it.

Some years ago I made an analysis of the "free
list" with a view to showing the farmer how much
he had to be thankful for. The details I forget.
I was,—I think,—on the whole a little disappointed. But I did find that the free list included then the items of false teeth, bibles, nux
vomica and grave-clothes. I drew the farmer's
attention to the fact that if he were discontented
he could set in his false teeth and read his bible,
then take a drink of nux vomica. There is now
a tariff on nux vomica, I believe. But that
doesn't matter. I see that "dragon's blood" is
free: so is "cyanide of potassium" and that's

quicker than nux vomica. Nor can he any longer
have his false teeth: not if they are "mounted".
But he can have an artificial leg instead. On his
coffin he pays 25 per cent. The Western farmer,
in a word, can put on his grave-clothes, prepare
for death and slip his tariff harness. But while he
lives, he pays.

It is true that the farmer of the Canadian West
is himself protected by an agricultural tariff. We
maintain a duty of 30 cents a bushel on wheat
from the United States (if it comes from England
it's free, along with the cyanide); oats 16 cents;
flour 50 cents a bushel, and so on.

But an agricultural tariff as between two
countries both agricultural and agricultural in the
same way is more or less a delusion. It is like
the dividing wall often used to separate a reser-
voir into two parts. with the water at the same
level on either side. The pressure is nothing.
Compared with this a tariff on manufactures is
like the wall of a dam holding back the upper
water twenty or thirty feet high at a pressure that
never relaxes. The agricultural tariff of Canada,
as a "seasonal" tariff to protect the Ontario market
gardener from over-early asparagus and such, is a
reality. Applied to the Western farms it is, as the
confidence men used to say, "Just good enough
for farmers."

*   *   *   *   *

Those of us of the older generation were all
brought up on the Victorian doctrine of free trade
as a sort of gospel. Protection was not only mis-

taken, it was immoral. Indeed it only came back
onto the modern world, after Cobdenism ended,
under a mantle of sin. The United States accepted it, and excused it, as a consequence of the Civil
War. Sir John A. Macdonald and the government
of 1878 accepted it as a consequence of the United
States. But it was not till the end of the nineteenth century, in the days of organized labour,
that protection (see the Republican platform of
1888) could stand on its own feet. Protection to
labour against the cheap living and low wages of
foreign countries is a sound doctrine, as sound today as ever.

But in Canada, unless we readjust, the whole
thing is a misfit. In the East there are ever so
many people interested directly or indirectly in
maintaining protective duties, huge industries such
as the automobile and implement industries: whole
towns that are tariff towns like Oshawa and
Windsor: farming areas around them interested in
the "home market" of their own centre more than
in selling to the foreigner. And most of all the
great cities are the home of what the Bolsheviks
call the "parasitic classes",—i.e., the professors,
the clergy, the actors and the lawyers. All these
people need for their jobs the big crowded city,
and as the tariff fosters the big city, they are all
for the tariff. Not for them the big open spaces.
No minister wants to be alone under God's sky:
the professor needs his class, the lawyer his criminals and the actor his gallery.

*   *   *   *   *

Take it in the most selfish way you like, with no appeal to general patriotism, most of the East favours the tariff, take it the same way and all the West is against it.

I do not think that the situation can be remedied by violent changes of policy, now this way now that, in response to a changing popular vote. I think that we have got to start, not with theory but at the other end. We have got to indicate a goal of fixed policy to be achieved and then find how to achieve it: this is the new method of administration,—find something impossible to do and then do it.

The object to gain is that the Western farmer in Canada need pay no more (minor fluctuations disregarded) than the United States farmer across the line for his motor car (on the prairie not a luxury but a necessity), for his agricultural implements and for such primary needs as shirts and boots and shoes. Till that is achieved there can never be political peace in Canada. Do it with free trade and you kill the cities of the East. But it can be done otherwise, by general subsidizing of the industry to equalize home and foreign costs. We have in Canada sometimes made steps in the direction of this system of bounties (the iron bounty of fifty years ago), etc., but we never went far. At first sight it seems to make all the people pay money on behalf of some of the people: the people with no cars pay for the cars of other people. But the objection loses weight when the commodities concerned are as universal as motor cars,

or implements used to raise bread and meat. The
principle of "distributing the burden" is one of
the newest and best of our economic doctrines; we
apply it wholesale to debt, to poor relief, to
medicine: there is no reason why it should not
apply to production.

To what extent this applies to boots and shoes
and clothes and prime necessities, I do not pretend
to say: there perhaps, a large extension of the nux
vomica list might be effected. Taxing a man's
shirt and pants is a dangerous process; tax his hat
and his gloves and his necktie if you will,—but his
shirt and pants,—risky.

In any case there are signs that the problem
will soon solve itself. Prices on the two sides
of the frontier will tend to be equalized by the
rise in the manufacturing costs under the labour
protection of the New Deal in the United States.
This reorganization of industry is admirable in
its general outline. It is at present hopelessly en-
tangled in the confusion created by the appeal to
the Supreme Court, a senile survival of legislative
method, admirable for George Washington, fatal
now when a nation must have economic unity or
crash. We too shall adopt it later: but in our
country, newer industrially and with less of a sub-
merged labour class, the effect on costs will be far
less and will be more than offset by the increasing
scale of manufacture.

*   *   *   *   *

But let it pass at that. There are lots of other
grievances as well. I turn to the vast burden of

debt,—provincial, municipal and private, under which the West has been in the last year or two literally crushed. It is my reasoned opinion that the debt as it stands cannot be carried, that a lot of it is unjust in its origin, some of it usurious to the verge of criminality and the whole burden of it intolerable. If it couldn't be brought down in any other way, it should be brought down with an axe like Jack in the Beanstalk's beanstalk. But I think it can be brought down, to within tolerable limits, by means that are not extraordinary or revolutionary but reasonable and, if the word is not offensive, conservative. Here are the large broad facts about debt in the West.

The situation just before the repudiation and readjustment begun in 1935 was like this. The bonded public debt of Manitoba just after the War (1919) stood at $36,000,000; in the year 1934 it had reached $90,000,000. In Saskatchewan the provincial debt during the same period moved from $29,000,000 to $112,000,000, and that of Alberta from $34,000,000 to $129,-000,000. Meantime the municipal debts of the provinces rose on a similar, if smaller, scale,— those of the Manitoba municipalities from $55,-000,000 (in 1933) to $96,000,000; for Saskatchewan the rise was from $39,000,000 to $57,000,000; and for Alberta from $57,000,000 in 1920 to $78,000,000 in 1931 with a reduction after that till 1933.

The comment of the Canadian Year Book of 1936 on the situation thus created, runs: "As a result of accumulated borrowings to meet conditions peculiar to the depression, the relentless advance of interest charges against realizable taxation has brought about a situation in many municipalities where expenditures are out of all proportion to receipts."

*   *   *   *   *

It must be remembered, however, that this aspect of Western debt,—the growth of provincial and municipal borrowing and the increasing pressure on ratepayers, has been parallel in all the other provinces of Canada. But there is a great difference. In the East a lot of the money has been borrowed from ourselves, in the West very little: we in the East are debtors and creditors both: in the West nearly all are debtors and hardly any creditors. In other words,—in the East we are debtors and creditors all in a heap with some lucky enough to sit up on top along with the American and British capitalist. In the West they are all in the heap and the Easterners sit on top of them along with the outsiders.

This is common knowledge. It would be hard to prove it with figures. The government of Canada officially estimated that over 62 per cent. of the debts and investments in Canada is held in Canada. This is mostly Eastern money.

But more important, more vital to the individual life and fortunes, is the piling up of private debts, and in especial of farm mortgages that reached a point where repayment of principal and interest was impossible. Accurate statistics here

66MY DISCOVERY OF THE WEST

are difficult to obtain. Even the census of 1931, much of which must represent pre-depression information, shows a black enough picture. In Manitoba 39 per cent. of the owners of farms who reported had mortagages. The mortgages averaged $10.00 per acre and the land was worth only $21.00. Saskatchewan and Alberta had 46 and 39 per cent. of owners with mortgages, but the debt less heavy per acre,—8 dollars out of 21, and 9 dollars out of 24.

But the rapid spread of debt, like a black cloud covering all the sky, is seen in such later documents as the questionaire answered in 1932 by 408 Saskatchewan farms that showed debts of principal and unpaid interest of $7,588 per farm or $16.88 for each acre of field crop.

A member of parliament told the House of Commons at Ottawa in 1932 that 81 per cent. of the Western farms were mortgaged and had a debt of over $4,000 per farm. The weight of the depression debt pressed in all directions. Manitoba, (as reported by the Social Service Council of Canada), lost between 1928 and 1930, no less than 36 per cent. of its rural telephone subscribers, Saskatchewan more than 40 per cent. and Alberta over one-half. School districts, villages and rural municipalities went broke. In 1932 they owed the banks over $8,000,000: the arrears of taxes impossible to collect was over $3,000,000.

This was the "glorious West' 'thrown open in the Jubilee year of 1897 as the "Granary of the

Empire: Free Homes for Millions: God Bless the Royal Family".

*   *   *   *   *

Now comes the Minister of Agriculture and tells us in his speech to parliament of February 11, 1937, that Saskatchewan all in all, province, town and district has a public debt of $600,-000,000.   One thinks back,—How did it all happen?   How came such a debt?

The West is largely, overwhelmingly, a farming community.   Only those who have lived on a farm know how easily a farmer gets into debt. It comes as the result of bad times: it also comes as the result of good times: it also arises from the introduction of improved machinery, better buildings, in short what is called agricultural progress.

Let me explain.   A farmer gets into debt owing to bad times, local and general.   His crops fail and he has to borrow money: or prices fall and he has to borrow money.   That's obvious.   But he also gets into debt through good times.   Good crops and rising prices mean that he can now build a new barn, with cowstables in a stone basement, build a brick house, put in a windmill, buy a motor car.   These things tempt a farmer as a silk dress tempts a debutante.   And naturally he builds even beyond his immediate ready cash: on goes a mortgage that at first sits as lightly as a straw hat. Then came the hard times and the mortgage crushes down like an iron extinguisher.   There it is, and there it stays, with its annual call for a hundred dollars interest spelling the difference between ease and anxiety. Drive along any well worn highway in older Ontario and look about you at the brick houses in the homesteads behind the spruce trees. What are those? Those are the mortgages left over from the Crimean War, when wheat sold at two dollars and a half a bushel. Or see the big tin barns with the "hip" roof of corrugated iron and under it the cattle stable, a real one, not the filthy unventilated shed that the mortgage drove away. A farmer in his stone basement with his cattle all end to end, feels as comfortable as I do in my library with all my books in a row. So arose the mortgages of the middle eighties and beside them the windmill mortgages, and the electrical mortgages for getting debt out of electricity. Of course if the farmer built only what he could pay cash for,—but then he knows that, as well as you do. And in any case you can't go backwards. Farmers who drive in motor cars and listen to radio, live under electric light and turn on a tap to water a cow, can never go back to the dim effulgence of coal oil, the jolt of the buckboard, and the slopping water of the barnyard pails freezing on both his legs at once. The clock won't turn back. It is machinery or nothing.

Nor do people always understand the brutal conditions under which farmers often have to borrow. Interest when it is really interest is fair enough: when it passes into usury it is criminal. And it belongs among those criminal acts, like poisoning and child kidnapping, as distinguished

from the violent blow of sudden anger, that ex-
cites the peculiar loathing of mankid. Interest in
the real sense corresponds to the fair return
upon money, the physical return on goods, the
"growth" of all animate nature. Usury is just
the turn of the screw of necessity.

The West had its share of debt, debt fairly in-
curred in what seemed an open market: and usury
all the more hateful in that it hid behind companies and agents and lawyers: not Shylock but
the Venetian Benevolent Association. Show me
a rich man who draws his money from the second-
mortgage of the poor and I'll show you a first
class skunk.

But quite apart from usury, the debt situation
in the West was intensified by the continuous fall
in prices, as oil is fed to a flame. Farm product
prices as between the normal year 1926 and the
deep depression year 1932 fell from 100 to 48,
including a fall in grain prices from 100 to 41.
This doubled the burden of mortgage interest.
"On a farm loan of $2,000 made at 8 per cent. in
1928,"—the words were those to the House of
Commons at Ottawa on April 11, 1932,—"the
interest would be $160.00 payable in 133 bushels
of wheat: in 1931 it would still be $160.00 but
payable with 266 bushels of wheat."

Incidentally one notices the "8 per cent." quiet-
ly quoted as regular and common interest. A rate
that would give a shudder to an Eastern debtor,
and make an Eastern shareholder smack his lips,
was taken by the Western farmer, as Eli Perkins

said he took the strokes of lightning, "on his bare back without a whimper."

So that is how debt came to Western Canada, at first with a touch so light and soothing it seemed like a healing hand; later like a dead weight that pressed everything down, sunk it deeper and deeper in the shifting miasma of the hollows of the depression.

The exultation of the West turned to a cry of despair. "As far as our Western agriculture is concerned," so pleaded to our House of Commons one of its prairie members, "unless some drastic measures are taken very soon, we shall have the bulk of our farmers in such an insolvent state that even under better conditions they can never hope to recoved their title of ownership of their farms."

That was on February 9th, 1932. It was already too late. We in the East had no ears to hear it: we too were sinking into the abyss, with everywhere unemployment, loss of salary, vanishing capital. We could do nothing. But now we must: and we must do it together.

Later on elsewhere in this volume I propose to discuss in detail the alleviation of Western debt. Much has been done in Saskatchewan already, where a reduction of $75,000,000 in farmers' debt was effected on a basis of compromise in the autumn of 1936. Much, if not overmuch, has been done in Alberta. In all the provinces the Farmers' Creditors Arrangement Act of the Dominion of Canada (1934), is alleviating without compulsion, many individual cases. But I think

that ever so much more can be done for all
debters and creditors without repudiation or com-
pulsion by consolidating a portion of Dominion,
provincial, and municipal debt, pro rata, under a
national guarantee with ear-marked revenue from
the province and the municipality. That would,
I think, at once cut the interest on that part of the
debt. Straight usury should be killed as we used
to kill snakes under a brush heap; add up the
usurious interest and, if its enough, call the debt
off. The rest of the debt can be left to the effect
of rising prices, renewed immigration and better
times. The sunshine of prosperity will lick it up
like rain in puddles.

I say renewed immigration, though I realize
that the word "immigration" drives many people
frantic. Labour, with only one eye, and academic
understanding with only one ear, cannot see and
hear properly. They think that each new immigrant takes away exactly one job from a man on
the spot. That's only true in the pit of depression. In good times each immigrant brings new
jobs for those on the spot. With him comes
money, capital, building, transport,—a whole
apparatus of bread and work for all. If this is
not so, let's get out one by one and leave the last
man with all Canada to romp in.

*   *   *   *   *

But the rest of the bill of grievances, the "money
power" (if there is one), the banks, and whether
people's credit is an improvement on bank credit,
I leave over till I come to deal with Sunny Alberta.

CHAPTER FIVE

SASKATCHEWAN AND WHEAT

How the Lord Made Saskatchewan—And
Made it a Wheat Farm—Agriculture and Machinery—The Wheat Problem—Impossibility
of Restricting Production—Means of Solution.

To appreciate the present position of the Pro
vince of Saskatchewan it is necessary to understand the process by which the Lord made it.
Countless ages ago the land surface of the globe
came heaving up, dripping from under the universal water. Above it was the dense cloud and
mist of the firmament such as still covers the planet
Venus. There was a half darkness called day, and
a total blackness called night. No stars shone and
there was no eye to see them. As the solid land
heaved up it was bent and buckled in great ridges
and furrows such as the vast upheaval that we call
the Rocky Mountains of America. Elsewhere, for
lack of room, it tilted up at the side, and bent into
slopes of rock, some this way and some that, like
the great rim round the Hudson Bay. Everywhere the water poured off like rain from a roof,
and it poured again in the rain flood from the
firmament. There was a universal roar of water
and no ear to hear it. As the water rushed in
streams it cut and tore at the primeval land, broke
it, pounded it from lumps to mud and spread it
out wider and wider, and wore channels through
it as the subsiding flood ran away. On the
mountain edges the channels formed great gorges.

On the broad slopes they form wide valleys
through which a broad flood poured with a lessen-
ing volume till it was a little stream in a valley so
wide as not to be recognizable,—such are the
broad valleys, the rolling ranges about the little
tributaries of the Qu'Appelle and the Assiniboine.
But elsewhere all the driven soil was piled up, as
the flood carried it, into thickened hills, and then
the water drove a deep curving hollow through it,
as a child's finger might be drawn through a mud
pie.   Such is the great valley of the South Saskatchewan as seen at Saskatoon.   And when the
land was all drained and the main flood gone, the
clouds cleared and the sun shone out, and then, in
the sunshine, mile after mile, rolling to the very
horizon was Saskatchewan.   Here and there as
the land dried out, great clouds of dust from the
broken sandstone of the hills came blowing across,
shifting and twisting like the sandhills of the
Sahara.   Such are the sandstreaks, and sandhills
that outcrop and mingle with the soil that later
became the black alluvium of the prairie.

Then came Life, creeping out of the water to
the land, and then Nature the Seedsman, scattering
in sweeping handfuls the newly evolved seeds of
plants and trees.   All over the rolling stretches the
soil broke out into grasses and bright flowers that
bloomed and withered unseen for countless ages,
and with their death and putrefaction enriched and
blackened the rock-dust into deep loam, dying that
still more might live.

But the trees grew but little.   Elsewhere, as in

the country that later became Ontario, the trees, sheltered in the hollows, presently climbed the hills, like soldiers springing from a trench in a joint attack. Alone they could not start; together, each protected the other. Even now a single hemlock breaks in the wind and dies; a forest lives on its collected strength, shouldering off the storm.

On the prairie it is not so. The winter blizzard could tear and rip and up-root everything. Nothing could live but little birch and cotton-wood, and cypress trees, shuddering together in the coulees and the deeper valleys. Start them and shelter them, and the trees could grow. For witness, see all the beauty in the little woodland that surrounds the parliament house at Regina. Or see them in Missouri, where, within the white man's memory, rolling empty prairie has turned to waving woods. But elsewhere on the prairies trees never started. They were still-born children. Yet if we wish it so, all Saskatchewan that will grow wheat could turn to forest.

Thus did nature strike its balance of life and death on the prairies and leave them thus for ages and ages, changing with every season, but unchanging with the centuries. "Over the meadows that blossom and wither, rings but the note of the sea birds' song, only the sun and the rain come hither, all the year long,"—so sang the poet Swinburne of his Forsaken Garden. But he might have sung it of the prairies of Saskatchewan; for the birds, like all life, first came, blowing in from the sea, and with the birds the animals, evoluted to a great bulk, slow and graminivorous. Last of all came man, rare and precarious and wandering.

In great flat spaces nothing can live standing still. Life must be picked up on the march. Even the mind cannot live, and keep its balance, in the empty openness of limitless horizon. The story is as old as the steppes of Asia and the solitude of the Sahara, and was reproduced again when the mind of the settler's wife kept breaking down in the fixed, empty stillness of an isolated homestead. Nothing but the blessing of the motor car, the ability to drive everywhere and nowhere, has supplied the same necessity that the Arab finds in his camel and a sailor in the motion of his ship. Motor cars, and more trees, to block here and there the empty horizons and to stop its suggestion of infinity,—that's all that's needed.

But human kind in the West before the white man came to America must have been infinitely rare, as far as the vast open prairie was concerned. Men couldn't live there. Not till the Spaniards brought the horse to America, and the wild horses multiplied, could mankind invade, in any real fashion, the open plains; and even then rather in annual raids and inroads than in fixed settlement. This was the 'buffalo and hunters' stage; the lost paradise of the half breed living under the rule of the great Company. Then came the settler to the plains, with his acquired apparatus of civilization and his mechanism of agriculture. The Company rule ended, the homestead farmers invaded the West. The Lord said 'let there be wheat' and Saskatchewan was born.

All that has gone above is not poetry.   It is intended as a view of the economic basis of Saskatchewan.

The Great Western Plain, thus formed and fashioned, includes in Saskatchewan the lower half of the province from the international boundary to the North Saskatchewan River.   Beyond it is the broken country of lake and timber reaching to the barren lands, as yet scarcely explored, perhaps a repository of great mineral wealth.   The Great Plain thus fully prepared by the hand of the Lord and opened up by the hand of man, offered itself to the raising of grain by machinery as did few places in the world.   In the more highly civilized countries of Europe, diversified by hills and valleys and broken by woods and winding roads, nature forbade machine cultivation.   Grapes can climb mountains, but not wheat.   In Switzerland,—we have it on the high authority of Mark Twain,—a farmer is apt to fall off his farm.   In the flat plains of Europe,—Hungary and the Ukraine,—mankind, as far as invention went, had been asleep for centuries.   In the fertile flats of China they had invented nothing since the wheelbarrow.   Even in older Canada, machinery in agriculture is still impeded by hills, by the remains of bush and swamp, snake fences and stone piles, and the little seven-acre divisions they call fields.

With the gamut of inventions that ran from the reaper, the gangplow, the seeder, the thresher, the binder, the tractor and ended with the crowning glory of the "combine",—the West came into its own.

The summer prairies of Saskatchewan took on the aspect since familiar in pictures to all the world, vast miles of ripening grain waving in the sunshine, with flickering shadows of fleecy clouds blowing over it.   There are no longer the "unshorn fields, boundless and beautiful" that Cullen Bryant saw.   They are better than that.   The prairie has yielded itself to man.   These boundless fields murmur with life as the ripe grain sways and falls in its luxuriant death.

Thus opened up possibilities of cheap production,—cheap and easy, its cost a mere nothing, in time, a punctuated idleness.   It seemed too easy. Calculations on twentieth century agriculture (comparing it with the nineteenth) made in 1925 by the United States National Industrial Conference showed that a Western farmer with a tractor ploughed eight times as much land in a day as a farmer with a team; that one man could take care of 300 acres of wheat instead of the 50 acres of oats, hay, bush, hens and mortgage that kept him hustling in Ontario; that he could raise a bushel of wheat with 10 minutes work! (in place of the three hours of his grandfather) and, with only one man to help for one fortnight, he could harvest and thrash all the grain of 500 acres! And after that,—nothing to do.   What about a trip to California?

Not even the milkmaid "who poised a full pail on her head" and counted the chickens she was going to buy, indulged in rosier dreams than the Western farmer balancing on his head four quarter sections of land, a tractor, a combine, one hired man and the interest on a mortgage.

Think of it,—500 acres of wheat,—no, make it 1,000! Lots of them had that, and 30 bushels of wheat to the acre (call it more if you like: nature can do it: it's a dream price anyway): farmer's cost of production (Canadian government figures these, a Bulletin on Wheat Production in Saskatchewan,—they must be right), even including 15 cents of interest, only 78 cents a bushel and the home price not the Liverpool price, the home price,—anything from a dollar up and sometimes over two! Oh, boy! can you beat it; just figure that out! and then some,—it may be away bigger than that.

No more for us the winter desolation of the prairie, contrasting with its summer sunshine:— the empty windswept landscape, with all life still and dead at 40 below,—with a blizzard sweeping the frozen snow in eddying circles,—even the sunlight hard and cruel with blindness in its empty stare. Away from all that! The sunny South, the laughing Pacific with its mermaids for us!

For some of them in those far off days the dream actually came true: they wrote their names on the hotel registers of California, like the foremost line of a charge that is beaten back.

But not many. For most of them this vision of a promised land vanished as it did for all of us. They just had a look over the fence and then somehow the promised land grew dim, grew distant and shifted as far away as ever. Man's servant machinery once so skilful and subservient had gone silly.

What went wrong?   The same thing as all over the world in all machine industries among people depending on buying and selling.   The machine went out of gear.   We are still tinkering to adjust it.   It looks just now as if by pure accident it is going to start up again with a roar! If so, Heaven knows we didn't do it!

The case of the farmers was this.   In the golden days all was well with the Western farmer except the selling of the wheat.   He wasn't sure that he got all that was coming to him: no matter what he got he might have got more.   It's an awful thought.   Anybody who has sold mining stock at a profit knows it.

The wheat price is made (makes itself) in the great European markets centering chiefly at Liverpool, and is reflected from thence to the markets of supply.   From 1900-1915 the Canadian price showed an average of 69 cents a bushel.   In the War years all the wheat was bought at a fixed government price, which was good and plenty (1917: $2.81—1918: $2.92).   Even after the War and when the War Board ceased to function, the price still held (1919-1923 average $1.83). But it was falling from the peak of $3.43 in 1919 to 98 cents in 1923.

Now this Canadian farmer's price is only a part of the Liverpool price which has to cover also a large series of charges for transport, storage and subsidiary services.   It is estimated that on each bushel there is 1¾ cents to pay for local elevator charges, 1 cent for a Winnipeg Broker, 15 cents rail to Fort William, 12½ cents Fort William elevator, 8¼ cents lake freight, 2 cents for Montreal handling, 6½ cents (variable) for ocean freight, in all, with varying details, about 45 cents.

This means that there are a number of people,— brokers, buyers, elevator men, railways, ships, banks,—trying to get as much of the "farmer's money",—that's the way they see it,—as they can. Any increase in their share makes his less. Any distribution of these costs shunts back on the farmer as a shock runs through a string of empty grain cars.

In the beginning the farmer was helpless. He owned no elevator, no railway. But, on the plains in early years, the wonder and gladness was to be able to *sell* at all. Red River farmers in the Fort Garry days could raise wheat but they had to *eat* it.

To get a better share farmers built elevators; so did the railways: brokers organized as the (Winnipeg) Grain Exchange: banks lent money on stored wheat. The Dominion government legislated on inspection, grading, marketing. A huge network, complicated in its outline and ramifying in its relations, spread out from the Head of the Lakes to the confines of the grain country. You can view it either as a thing of beauty or of horror, a work of God or of the devil, according to the type of mind you have. But at least it was intricate. If it ever burst there was bound to be an awful crash.

The final step was the formation of the pools, one in each Prairie Province with a joint connection through a central sales agency, the Canadian Cooperative Wheat Producers Limited, Winnipeg. Thus the word "Pool", while this situation lasted was often used as a collective name for the three of them. The essence of a pool is this:—in the old days the farmer sold his grain as soon as he had threshed it and was presently sorry he had sold it. Under a "pool" the farmer can hold his grain till later, and perhaps presently be sorry that he didn't sell it. But there is at least this difference: the old farmer *had* to sell: the pool farmer doesn't. It's like "predestination" and "free will".

Under the pool system, as it developed, each member was pledged to sell his wheat by and through his provincial pool: the central agency acted for them all and became itself a member of the Winnipeg Grain Exchange. The farmer received an initial payment of so many cents per bushel plus interim payments (for example in the first year of the pool operation 1924-25 he got one dollar and sixty-six cents in all). The pools were agents only: they distributed no profits on the nominal shares but made a small charge to cover expenses (half a cent a bushel), two cents for a fund for building Pool Elevators, and one per cent. reserve.

In the years of sunshine the system worked

admirably. So do most systems. But it lead
to serious misunderstandings. People began to
think that the Western pool could "control" the
price,—make it go higher. This it couldn't do.
The pool could use its joint resources and its power
to borrow from the banks to *hold* wheat and not
throw it on the market at a bad time. But that is
all. If the market is bad enough the longer you
hold the more you lose. It is as if you clutched a
share of stock tight in your hand, tighter and
tighter, and presently opened your hand to find it
gone to dust. No conjurer is needed for that. So
it was with the farmer and his pool.

The world wheat stock is too large, its consti-
tuents too varied, its potential increase too great,
to allow for any such cornering. Canada is a
wheat country but there are others. Our 250,000
farmers in the West are only a part of the millions of farmers in the world. Before this century
began, Canada as a wheat-producing country was
just nowhere. The world's crop around the year
1900 was some 2,640,000,000 bushels: of this
Russia grew 424,000,000 bushels, the United
States 600,000,000; a group of countries, France,
Hungary, etc., about 300,000,000 each. Great
Britain raised 52 million bushels and Canada only
50 millions. The Canadian export of wheat was
negligible. The "Granary of the Empire",—the
phrase of 1897,—was an expression of hope not
of fact.

Since the War Canada has raised huge crops of
wheat. The largest year's crop was seen in the

year 1928 with over 560 million bushels. Yet
the Canadian crop only represents about ten per
cent. of the largest world crop (that of 1932),
while the Canadian wheat crop of the drought
year of 1935 was less than 8 per cent. of an average
world crop.

Taking the average annual production of wheat
for the years 1929-30-31-32-33,—the world's
crop was 3,707,000,000 bushels. There were 37
countries (21 of them in Europe itself) which
averaged more than 5,000,000 a year. The Canadian average, 354,000,000, was below that of
Russia 839,000,000, of the United States 783,-
000,000; only just above that of India 350,-
000,000 and of France 305,000,000, and closely
followed by Italy 258,000,000, and the Argen-
tine 228,000,000.

It is true that if one takes account of wheat
export in place of the amount of wheat *grown,* the
situation appears at first sight vastly different.
Canada has become since the War the leading
wheat-exporting country of the world. During
the time between the end of the War and the great
collapse, Canadian wheat sold abroad represented
35 to 40 per cent. of all exported wheat: the same
is still true in the dislocated and spasmodic world
trade of today. The Canadian export of 1935-36
was 47½ per cent. of the world total export.

But this does not, as it well might with other
commodities, imply a power to squeeze or force the
market. All the other world-wheat is there as a
potential export if the price is forced up. There

was no real economic basis for the hope of many Western farmers that the establishment of a "100 per cent. compulsory pool" would of necessity allow a lift of the export price.

With the turn of the times came a collapse of wheat prices at the very period when successive years of drought lessened the volume of the Canadian crop. Winnipeg wheat (No. 1 Hard), the best in the world, showed disastrous prices,—64 cents for 1929-31, 59 cents for 1931-32 and 54 cents for 1933-34.

Under such repeated shocks the Western pools practically went under: with fallen membership and diminished sales, the collective selling of the central agency came to an end: the pools, existing still, own elevators and handle and forward grain but the system, as it was designed, is over. With the fall of wheat there spread over the West the tidal wave of mortgage and farm debt with which the provinces now struggle as best they can by means of statutes of repudiation in Alberta, of debt reduction in Saskatchewan and with the aid of the Dominion Farmers' Creditors Adjustment Act.

The establishment by the Dominion government of a Wheat Board (under an act of 1935) merely offers facilities for sale if the price drops enough with no organization of cooperative marketing. The experiment has finished its opening stage and the time is ripe for reconsidering wheat policy in Canada,—the whole question of production, of possible restriction, of open trading, or collective action.

Here it must be understood that our wheat situation is only a part of a world phenomenon,— the over-production, the economics of abundance, that has resulted from the progress of machinery and organization. There is no need to discuss the details of it here. Everyone has heard of the car loads of melons floating down the Potomac, the stocks of burning coffee in Brazil, and of the unborn hogs and unplanted corn of the American Middle West.

The world at large will somehow, sometime, find a means to limit production to what people can buy, or conversely to enable people to buy all that other people can produce. But the wheat of the export market at present utterly defies such restriction. It is possible to limit production where nature's supply is small and gathered in one place. The production of diamonds has been restricted for a generation. Production can be limited even for large scale commodities if the supply can be got at and held and if common labour alone cannot increase it: such is the case of rubber. Or if the production demands great capital and corporate organization, even the hugest output can be controlled by company agreement: coal, iron, and steel, vast as they are, can be controlled. Or inside a closed area (as with the hogs in Mr. Roosevelt's America) production can be restricted by law. If Mr. Roosevelt won't let hogs in, and won't let the extra hog get born, then nature is brought to a full stop. But wheat! that will grow, more or less well, all through the north and the south temperate zone, that can be grown in a dirt heap with a stick, that has behind it in Western Canada alone 250,000 independent producers, and elsewhere millions and millions. Restriction is just a dream.

If we don't grow wheat others will. It is inevitable,—it is a provable economic proposition, that the world's wheat production is bound to run to over-production and temporary collapse. Sound national policy must take that for granted and contrive to bridge the gaps and not let the temporary collapse of the price mean permanent ruin to the farmers.

What we ought to do in Canada is to take over from the individual farmer the worst of the risk of raising wheat. I say wheat because it is the major crop, governing all others. I do not know to what extent, if at all, the argument applies to other grains. If we guarantee too much we insure our own damnation by subsidizing the farmer to ruin us. If we guarantee too little, the farmer is ruined anyway. If a man is ruined he doesn't care if he owes $100 and can't pay it, or $1,000 and can't pay it. We must guarantee a rock bottom price for wheat that is enough, just enough to keep the farmer on the farm, without a mortgage,—his motor car rattling in every joint, his trip to California up the flue, perhaps his radio cold and silent,—but still on the farm. As to the world's crop, let it look to itself: for the present there is no other way.

Many people, especially those brought up on

farms in Eastern Canada, are apt to wonder why the West cannot find salvation by transforming its agriculture from grain farming to mixed farming. The semi-independent homestead of the East, like the small holdings of the French cultivators, offer a bulwark against disaster: less productive in the money sense, they are more human in their interest, safer against changes of price and circumstance, and more solid and enduring as the basis of civil society.

Opinion in the West overwhelmingly tells us that the cases are not parallel. For the West it is mechanized farming or nothing. The great plains are lacking in water, in wood, in diversity. The very suitability for vast fields of wheat forbids other uses. It is true that in the new areas of the Peace River and even to some extent in the northern half of Saskatchewan, as yet hardly occupied, there may be room for barnyard and woodpile farming. It is true that a rearrangement of holdings to favour communal pasturage and bring dwelling houses in closer range may at once diversify agriculture and social life. But in the main the economic future of the prairie country must follow the fortune of machine agriculture. It has made its bed and must lie in it; and its couch not the trim bed of a vegetable garden but the "boundless and beautiful" field from which it took its name.

All that can be done, then, is to go ahead and raise wheat like all possessed.

But for the next few years,—four or five,

and who cares to look further,—there is a plan that has occurred to me for which I have already solicited a little publicity. The idea is that of storing up in England, as a war measure, enough wheat, or flour, to last five years even if all supplies are cut. It would mean, I think, about 1,000,000,000 bushels,—call it that anyway. It is harder to store wheat in England than it is here owing to the damp climate. But modern scientific refrigerator methods, and "conditioned air" can make a sport of all that. Wheat shrinks, I understand, about 1 per cent. in its first year, after that very little. But what it loses is only water, and there's lots of that.

It would be a great thing if England would buy all our export crop for a few years for this purpose: a greater thing, still, if we *gave* it to them, or at least a lot of it. We could do it as our contribution to imperial defense.

The Canadian Parliament is opening up a debate on imperial and national defense. It is a dangerous discussion. The attempt to show that we need to join in Empire defense may lead people to pretend that we need defense here. as against the Americans.

That is just crazy and worse. That could do infinite harm. Our best defense, our only defense, against the Americans, and theirs against us, is to have no defense at all. None that either of us could ever prepare would be effective along such a frontier. We live in peace or die together.

We show every sign of living in peace. Don't

let's spoil it by pretending that we need air-bases and gas masks and sally ports and demi-culverins and half-scotches against the Americans. We don't. Honestly, I wouldn't shoot an American, even if I found him sitting on a bough where I could sneak right up on him.

So the idea which I propose is as large as the side of a house, in fact as large as the side of a grain elevator.

Let us make our Empire contribution in the shape of a huge annual gift of wheat for storage in England against war. England must begin to store up wheat, flour, oil and food in this cursed situation that has arisen.

If we give them wheat it is as good as gunpowder. The beauty of it is that it has all the Scotch virtue of being a mighty canny thing for ourselves anyway. It would be the end of all this "carry-over" trouble, this "nonproduction" and "go easy". It would mean that merry old Saskatchewan would put on so many teams and so many tractors for spring plowing on such a big scale that they'd disappear over the horizon.

CHAPTER SIX

OUR ELDORADO IN THE WILDERNESS

The Wilderness that Divided Canada—An Unsuspected Aladdin's Cave—Its Mineral Wealth—Canada and Gold—Proper Uses of a New Gold Standard.

In the centre of Canada, running in a great sickle, or crescent, around the Hudson Bay, is what long seemed to be a vast wilderness of rock and scrub and muskeg, doomed to hyperborean cold, sterile and silent. Even where the silence was broken by the roar of falling waters, the tumult was only a meaningless fury of foam, useless for transport or commerce.

In our own immediate day all this is changed, this barren wilderness is now our Eldorado. From the Flin-flon mines on the border of Saskatchewan to the Belcher Islands off the mouth of the Great Whale River, it is now one vast Aladdin's cave. It is the greatest mineral district of all the world. Beside its vast deposit the Comstock lode is just a pocket, Ballarat a memory and even the Witwatersand only a beginning. Here is gold with silver and copper as bye-products, or copper and zinc with a bye-product of casual gold. Here is nickel, the delight of the God Mars and of his humble servant the Tubal Cain who once made iron ploughshares now makes hard-metal castings. Over these thousands of miles of wilderness aero planes float in the sky and flurry on the frozen lakes, carrying a new race of men, as Hyperborean as the cold itself.

This new Eldorado means for us the achievement of the long sought unity of Canada. Gold means, when we know how to turn it to the magic of currency and credit, the alleviation of the burden of debt, the restoration of prosperity. It is all there. Nothing needed but brains and unity of purpose.

*   *   *   *   *

The main importance to us of this central Eldorado, we repeat, is not the commercial value in gold and metals but the effect it is destined to have. is having already, on the unity of Canada. Till recent times Canada seemed hopelessly cut in two in the middle. The downward sweep of the Hudson and James Bays reduces its north-and-south mainland dimension from 1,500 miles to little more than 300. Worse than that,—the Hudson and James Bays are, to all intents, land-locked seas: they are not, like the other seven seas of the temperate zone, a means of commercial access. Otherwise a new Vancouver might arise at Churchill or at the Ontario tide-water harbour of Moosonee. The one ship a year sent through the Straits by the Hudson's Bay Co. for two centuries, hardly counts except as romance. Neither do the grain ships of the last five years since the Hudson Bay Railway and the Churchill port were opened in 1931. Up-to-date the route has cost $70,000,000 and has carried, in five years, 17,000,000 bushels of grain. Neither do the odd whalers count, in days when Hudson Bay whales are getting as doubtful as Jonah. Worse than that: there are no smaller fish in the Bay, or none to speak of. This was a peculiar piece of hard luck for British North America. With fish in the Hudson Bay, to compare with those of the Grand Banks and the North Sea, a new Aberdeen could have arisen, college and all, at the mouth of the Rupert or the Great Whale.

But the worst feature of all was the character of the land itself. All the way around the great bay, along what is now the sea-coast of Manitoba, Ontario, and Quebec, stretched a frozen wilderness of rock, leading nowhere, of unending forests of small and worthless trees, broken with sunken muskeg, and ending in a low and mournful sea coast, shallow for miles out, fringed with ice in winter and wild, from its very shallowness, with equinoctial storms, Over this hyperborean region brooded the eternal cold. As late as in the year 1866 (the year before Confederation) a "new edition" of *Lippincott's Philadelphia Gazetteer* could write: "There can be but little doubt that the greater part of the vast region included under the name of British America is doomed to everlasting sterility on account of the severity of its climate." All Canadians are still familiar with Goldwin Smith's famous picture of Canada in his *Canada and the Canadian Question* of 1891. He shows it as a country divided into geographical sections, with wildernesses in between,—and the greatest of these, the wilderness of the Lake Su-

perior country.   It all seemed worthless.   The
rushing rivers meant nothing while electricity still
slept.   At Confederation, paper was still made
from rags: there was no such word as pulp-wood:
the spruce, too small for lumber. stood buried in
the snow, a billion Christmas trees without a
Xmas.   The best that any one could say of the
place was that it was a "sportsman's paradise",
which only means a good place to drink whiskey
in.

All that even geology could say was that this
great semi-circle of rock was the oldest part of the
globe, the first land that God made.   That was at
least an apology for it.

Yet it is a romance of our Canadian history that
the Indians knew, in a general way, about the
mineral district.   They tried to tell Jacques
Cartier about it on the top of Mount Royal in
1535, touching the silver whistle that he carried
and the copper of his dagger and pointing up the
Ottawa.   Hence the legend of the Kingdom of
"Sagné" or Saguenay which presently mixed up
its geography and shifted to the wrong place.   But
if Cartier could have reached the country beyond
the Ottawa and found silver (that he could re-
duce) the world's history would have been different.   Later on complacent historians said the
Indians only meant the silver waters of the
Ottawa.   Professors can explain anything.

Then came—all within forty years or so,—
accident and chance and invention—and changed
the wilderness into the place that we now know,

the greatest mineral district in the world, with hydro-electric power to run it, and with thousands of square miles of pulp-wood to turn into newspapers to talk about it.

*   *   *   *   *

It is not possible in this space (and without a change of writer) to describe in its geological and metalliferous aspect the watershed that forms the great "rim" around the Hudson Bay.   It is a vast country.   The sea coast of Ontario alone extends 680 miles.   To those of us who fully remember the limited Ontario of fifty years ago, this sounds like Shakespeare's "sea coast of Bohemia".   Manitoba has a coastal line of four hundred miles, while that of Quebec which extends "round and out" to the Atlantic, has at least an equal extent of the sea coast that is the mineral area.

The technical description of this mining area as given by an expert, for example, as explained by the Geological Survey Department for our admirable *Canadian Year Book,* sounds like Greek to most of us.   Yet it sounds fine too.   "The great area in Eastern Canada underlain by rocks of Precambrian age is known as the Canadian or Precambrian Shield.   It may be regarded as a peneplanated surface that has been rejuvenated by Pleistocene glaciation (fine!) . . . . The Precambrian formations are prolific of mineral deposits of great number, variety and extent. Among them are the gold deposits of Porcupine and Kirkland Lake, associated with intrusions of porphyry, the silver deposits of Cobalt, South

Lorrain and Gowganda, associated with diabase
sills, the enormous nickel-copper deposits of Sudbury associated with norite of a thick laccolithic
intrusion, the auriferous copper sulphides of western Quebec, and the copper zinc sulphides of
Manitoba ." Intrusions of Porphyry! It sounds
like King Solomon's Mines, the Building of the
Temple and the Queen of Sheba.

*   *   *   *   *

The increasing importance of mineral production in Canada is a notable feature of our national
economy. Since the first regular estimates made in
1886, the value of mineral production per capita
has risen from $2.23 to $28.33 in 1935. This is
chiefly owing to the discoveries in the Hudson and
James Watershed. Ontario alone produces over
50 per cent. of the minerals of Canada: Quebec
adds another 12 per cent. In gold Ontario produced in 1934 some 60 per cent. and Quebec 10
per cent. of the output. Taking the same year as
the latest for world comparisons, 81 per cent. of
the world's nickel, 13 per cent. of the copper, of
lead 12, of zinc 10, of silver 9, and of gold 11 per
cent.

The Canadian output of gold in several years
(1931-2-3) surpassed that of the United States
and was exceeded only by Russia and South
Africa. In 1934 it stood at 2,972,000 fine ounces,
with South Africa (10,479,000 fine ounces) leading Russia (4,262,000) and the United States
(2,741,000). The present Canadian output is
greater than that of California and Colorado

added together, and greater than they were in the golden legendary days of 1851 to 1855. It is an easy prophecy that Canada will soon rank second, and in a measurable time first among the gold countries.

The Canadian annual output of gold can be computed (see Jacob's *History of the Precious Metals*) at probably twice as much as all the gold existing in Europe in the days between Charlemange and Columbus in the year 1492. The gold and silver together only equalled about $160,-000,000 and silver was the far greater part. The feeble annual production just maintained the stock. The Canadian annual output of gold is twelve times as great as the "flood" of gold that came each year to Spain after the exploits of Cortes and the Pizarros and five times as great as all the world produced even when Queen Victoria began to reign. This steady rise in the production of gold heaps up an accumulated stock. Gold may be mislaid: it can't be destroyed. The $50,-000,000 (maximum) of 1492 had increased by 1935 to $21,500,000,000, using a fine ounce of gold to mean 20.67 "dollars" and counting only the gold in central banks and government reserves, and not the mass of gold hoarded and converted to ornamental and commerciad use.

Incidentally our new Canadian method of calculating the value of gold in our present depreciated paper dollar at $35.00 to the ounce distorts all appearance and makes riches out of poverty, like the reflection of a thin man fattened in a convex mirror. We ought to get away from it.

The steady rise in the stock of gold, faster than the rise in "business" has made the progressive increase in price a fixed feature of large-view history. As far as such a thing can be calculated, English prices at the end of Queen Victoria's reign were perhaps twenty times the prices of Norman England. This steady rise is of great meaning to Canadian public policy. If we keep to a gold standard, it will automatically lift a lot of our debt and automatically prime the pump of business.

But before talking specifically of gold, turn a moment to the sister metals of our Eldorado.

Here first is nickel. This is a metal, an element. It was known, like everything else, to the ancient Chinese; but they got nowhere with it. Europe knew nothing of it till the end of the eighteenth century when it was first completely separated from combined ore by the Swedish chemist Torbern Bergman. But it was a rare metal, indeed there was hardly any of it. A little turned up in metallic combinations in United States' mines, quite a lot on the island New Caledonia, the French penal settlement off Australia. Modern metallurgy learnt to use it towards the end of the nineteenth century. Mixed with iron and carbon it makes nickel-steel: with chromium added it makes nickel-chromium steel. These combinations are of great hardness: they constitute the armourplate and the great guns of war and enter into a hundred of its grim uses. Only 3 or 4 per cent. of nickel with less than 1 per cent. of carbon, or a little more than 1 per cent. of chromium, turns cheap iron into the implements of death. But nickel also stands for peace. The fault is ours if we think of it in terms of war. It is unique as a hardening alloy for castings, for highly-stressed forgings, for boiler plate, bridge steel, motor car parts and for plating, coin-making,—a thousand means of human happiness. Of the world's supply of this ambiguous product Canada contributes from 80 to 90 per cent. a year. It is found chiefly in New Ontario near Sudbury.

The nickel bearing rocks in the district form a sort of band or strip, over two miles wide, and running round in an ellipse about 36 miles long and 13 miles across the middle. Here is enough nickel "in sight" (as miners call things that can't see) to last the world for years and years, and probably lots more in the same wilderness.

In the last year fully reported (1934) the world used about 80,000 tons (2,000 lbs.,—the "short" ton) of nickel and Canada supplied about 70,000 tons of it. The value was about $35,-000,000 ($500 a ton, 25 cents a pound).

But nickel is only the most outstanding of these new element minerals not important in themselves but in the power contained in a small quantity of them to alter the temper or the properties of common metals, like iron, themselves easily obtained but only rudimentary in their use. Side by side with nickel in Canada is cobalt, an element metal used as an alloy, along with tungsten, in making

steel for the permanent magnets needed in telephones: and used along with tungsten and
chromium in making the hard steel of high-speed
cutting tools, that must be indifferent to heat. The
metal world of today includes as agents of vast
importance substances unknown or unheeded fifty
years ago: the vanadium brought from the summit of the Andes to make a 1 per cent. alloy
of effectiveness: radium, the world's mystery,
barium so strangely sensitive that in pure shape it
takes fire at the touch of water, molybdenum,—
things only names and mysteries to us humble
outsiders, and most of all to people of my generation who traded the opportunity to learn
"science" for a knowledge of the Greek verbs.
Some of these metals we have in Canada: some
not, or not as yet. Of cobalt we had, ten or
twelve years ago, all the world's supply—till it
turned up also on the Congo and elsewhere in
Africa. Radium we have,—besides the Great Bear
Lake, wisely and secretly held by the government
of Canada, being out of the clutches of the provinces. But it is likely that all the world's metals,
and enough of them will be found in our frozen
treasure house of the North.

Of all these, in history, in prestige, in commercial (not in intrinsic) value, gold takes first
place. But before talking of gold it is necessary
to make quite clear the way in which gold and
gold-standard-money was, and is, measured and
computed. This is all the more necessary now
that the standard is merely a piece of paper. Such

a majesty still hedges the idea of a "pound sterling" or a "U.S. dollar" that we don't realize that at present a pound sterling and a U.S. dollar are twin sisters to an Alberta Prosperity Certificate.

Gold is properly measured in "fine ounces" which means ounce weights of pure gold. The ounces are the so-called Troy ounce of 480 grains. The grains are combined into pennyweights or carats which contain 24 grains. Gold that is "18 carats fine" means gold mixed with alloy in the proportion of 18 to 6. It follows that 20 penny-weights make an ounce. But pennyweights and carats are only used in jewelers' reckoning, not in monetary science. The ordinary "ounce" of the butcher and baker is the ounce avoirdupois, con-taining 437½ grains. It is to be noted that a grain is a grain whether avoirdupois or Troy. It originally meant an ear of dried wheat. It now means the 7,000 part of the pound avoirdupois, which itself is an arbitrary standard based on a physical sample.

None of this sounds necessary but it all is.

A pound sterling (a sovereign), after meaning a lot of other things, came to mean (under the coinage act of 1816) and continued to mean until England went off the gold standard, a coin weigh-ing in all 123.27 grains and being 11/12 or .9166 pure gold, and 1/12 alloy.

Gold with this particular amount of alloy (1 in 12) was called standard gold or crown gold. An ounce of "standard gold", it follows from what has been said, would coin into rather less

than 4 sovereigns: to be exact, and using the
money divisions of the sovereign to mean frac-
tions, it would coin into £3-17-10½. Since
coinage at the mint (apart from a trifle charge for
assaying the metal) was free and unlimited, this
was the amount in money which the mint was
supposed to give for gold. Putting it in terms of
pure gold or "fine ounces" it corresponds to a
"value" of £4-4-11½ to the ounce. But this
"value" is not a price in the real sense. It is an
equation. It is like saying that 2 pints make a
quart. Many people were very silly, or confused,
over this, and now that the situation is mixed up
with paper they are sillier still. What made confusion a little pardonable was that in practice gold
in England was by the public taken not to the
mint but to the Bank of England. The Bank was
called upon to give £3-17-9 for standard gold.
The difference between this and the equation-value
represents the fact that immediate payment re-
moves the delay of coinage and hence is worth a
small item of interest. The Bank by law had to
pay this and *could* pay more. At times when,
for various reasons, the Bank wanted gold it paid
a little more, because the people bringing gold
didn't actually take away sovereign coins for the
full amount but accepted in whole or in part a
bank credit. So the Bank at times paid a little
extra, which gave the appearance of a fluctuating
"price of gold" in London (from £3-17-9 to the
full mint price).

The U. S. mint accepted unlimited gold in fine

ounces, mixed with alloy 1 part in 10 and made gold dollars (in pieces of 5, 10 and 20) which contain 23.22 grains of pure gold. This meant that a fine ounce of gold coined (with the alloy added) into $20.67. This meant again as a matter of arithmetic that the relative gold content, and hence the relative value of U. S. gold dollar and British gold sovereign (from 1836-1919) stood as 4.86 2/3 dollars to one sovereign. This was called the *mint part of exchange* and was the rate at which, other things being equal, people paid U. S. dollars to get British sovereigns. In practice things very seldom equal and wouldn't stay equal long. Either a surplus of people in America wanted to pay down dollars and have payments in England made in sovereigns or vice versa. At the "worst come to the worst" they could always send the actual gold across the ocean. But this costs money for transport, safe-keeping, insurance and interest on its being out of service for a week or so. It may be said that it costs almost four cents as a maximum to send one sovereign across the ocean. Hence an English or American person wanting a "draft" across the ocean would pay, if he had to, as much as 4 cents per sovereign to get it over, or be delighted to find it in the other way and find that his English sovereign would get him 4 cents extra in a draft expressed in U. S. dollars.

These up and down variations held in check by actual shipment of gold were called the "gold points" (4.82 2/3-4.90 2/3), and the fluctuation price of U. S. dollars and sovereigns was one of the "foreign exchanges". There were similar ones for francs, roubles, marks, etc., exchanged into dollars, pounds, etc. In Canada we used a gods-awful form of computation of which not even the bank clerks understood the original meaning, let alone the Bank Presidents,—and which was based on the percentage to be added to an older, heavier, imaginary gold dollar (the one of Halifax currency) to make the new dollars of 4.86 2/3 to the pound. The expression 9½ is par meant add 9½ per cent. to 4.44 and you get 4.86 2/3. In reality the bank clerk had a money table hanging beside him which told him all about it, till the rush of the exchange in August of 1914 bust his table. Since then we count as the Americans do.

Till the Great War, the open mint, the liberty to buy and sell, and import and export gold formed what was called the international gold standard. In the opinion of many people, of whom I am one, it was one of the greatest benefits to the world for a whole century. Automatically it moved gold from mining to non-mining countries: automatically, though more slowly and with friction, it kept tending to level world prices because high prices attracted goods and sent out domestic money, which tended to lower prices and contrariwise low prices attracted foreign gold. In both cases the foreign exchange supplied the mechanism. The broad general life of the world's commerce moved and breathed as with the slow heart beat of a great animal. Now it chokes, strangles and gasps for the air of monetary liberty.

The gold standard has in its time been passionately denounced. First of all it was denounced (in the later part of the nineteenth century) by labour, later by capital. In the nineteenth century, the expansion of business and the relative shortage of gold made low wages and depression. So it was argued: of the facts there was no doubt: of the causes there might be. Hence the cry of oppressed labour against gold. "You shall not," said Jennings Bryan in 1896, "press down upon the brow of labour this crown of thorns, you shall not crucify mankind upon a cross of gold". The cry, unhappily, echoes still when now the cross would mean, as crosses should, salvation.

Later on, in the post-war period, something of the same complaint has been raised by the economists. "The gold standard", so claims one of the least ignorant (one dare not say *most eminent* of economists), "is as antiquated as the stage coach". The metaphor is a favourite one of people without imagination who do not realize that the stage coach was murdered by the railway train and has now come back as its ghost,—the motor car,—to haunt the railway. "Coaches" blow their horns again from New York to San Francisco and from the Oasis of Timgad to Timbuctoo. But few economists ever had imagination.

What was meant was that the gold standard was *rigid,* and would mean, for lack of enough gold, a lowering of prices that would choke business, or, by superabundance of gold and of credit based on it, a burst of high prices that would turn business into a fever. What was needed, argued and still argue these people, was a *managed currency*, in which by manipulating the issue of credit-documents prices can be made to go up or go down and stay quiet and business be guided accordingly.

Let it be noted right here, with wide open eyes, that the phrase *managed currency* has quite recently been taken up in Western Canada in a sense utterly different from that used by London bankers and economists. What an Alberta farmer means by a "managed currency" is some system by which a decent man can borrow, if he has to borrow, on fair terms and get money to carry on and good prices for his crops and cattle,—manage that and he's satisfied. And little does he think that the despised "gold standard" offers us in Canada the means to do it. What the London banker and economist and financier mean, if you get down to brass tacks, is that the three of them will "manage the currency" by themselves in a closed room. If so I'd like to sit in with them and make it four. I'd undertake to come out rich. Talking in ideal terms, "managed currency" means that all dangerous inflation of credit will be carefully prevented, that dull business will be gradually strengthened, etc., etc. Among a set of omniscient angels, so it would be. With the world as it is, and with us as we are, I don't think it would be. It would just afford a new means in which the organized power of collective finance could act in its own interest. Money must be automatic or nothing. It must be a *fact*, like a beaverskin, or a roll of tobacco, or a goat, or a bit of paper actually convertible into a bit of metal.

At present it is not a fact at all. Notice what has happened. The English pound sterling is just a bit of paper. If you buy fine ounces of gold with it the "price" in paper is about 140 shillings, and goes up and down like the price of eggs. So with the U. S. dollar but worse. An act of Congress permitted the executive government to lessen the fine gold content of the dollar. It was declared lessened in January 1934 to 13.714 grains. But this dollar is just imaginary, it is never coined and never bought and sold. The one bought and sold is the *paper* dollar, and its price paid in it for an ounce of gold runs now at about $35.00. Thus the paper dollar price of gold per ounce is at present close to the price in imaginary Roosevelt dollars the imaginary coinage of the U. S. But it is not really connected with it: it is only sitting beside it. For proof look on the same tree and you'll see the Canadian dollar, another paper bird, sitting beside the American. Yet the Canadian dollar, not having been degraded, is still said to have a par of $20.67 to the ounce, still to contain 23.22 grains of pure gold.

Now the British government, through the Bank of England, keeps an imposing quantity of gold "behind" the paper, in 1935 about $1,600,-000,000 (old standard). And the United States a super-imposing sum "behind" its paper currency, about $10,000,000,000 of gold, reckoned in the old dollar of coinage. But this money is not for *redeeming* the paper. It is just behind it,—like Satan. Both countries use stabilization funds to act as a brake on a movement of the paper exchange: that is, the English government can cause vast sums of actual gold to be sold, or bought, and so can the American, and hence the dollars and the pound may be driven along like a carriage team. But a stabilization in reality is very limited in its ultimate power. It can stop speculators from trying to work the market. It can bridge a temporary gap in the national movement of commerce. But that is all. Behind it the tide of real commodities can sweep it away: it is only an *embankment* not a hill: it is a see-saw, not a sidewalk: the plate balanced on a juggler's chin, not a plate on a cupboard shelf.

Moreover the production of gold as a market commodity differs from that of everything else. The market is,—has been hitherto,—unlimited, since the product is money itself. The factor that counts is the amount payable in wages and costs; hence the harder the times, the lower the wages, the greater the profit of mining. The industry thrives on hard times, lives on depression. In the days of open mints, since the coined product was itself the medium of payment of wages and costs, this tendency kept trying to equalize itself in the long run: kept trying to run to an equation when it cost just about a dollar in gold wages, to produce

a dollar in gold metal; at any less cost the industry
would boom; at a greater cost it would slacken.
The huge accumulated world stock acted like
a fly wheel to prevent rapid alternations of speed
and slack.   But the tendency was there.

All this changes when gold is sold only for in-
convertible paper.   The market is still unlimited
but the more paper loses value the higher is the
relative value of gold.

Costs, and especially wages, do not fall as fast
as the gold value inflated does.   Hence under these
circumstances the industry enjoys a premium.
This is exactly what happened to Canadian gold
mining after the War as the paper value of gold
rose from $20.67 per fine ounce to $35.00 an
ounce.

It is true that our government "sets the price",
or thinks it does: but only in the sense that a
farmer "sets the clock". The farmer doesn't make
it *noon*: he only takes it from somewhere else.   So
our government merely estimates what it thinks
to be about the price in the world open market
and pays that sum for gold.

This stimulus on mining, if not carried too
far, is a wonderful thing for us.   It gives us a
vast and growing industry, induces private people
to incur the cost of exploration, and, as a bye-
product, opens up thousands of square miles,
makes railways possible, and brings the development of power.   The worst thing we can do is to
over-tax the gold mining industry.   A certain
amount of the bonus or premium that falls to it

from the good luck of the appreciation of gold, we may with propriety take away for the public use: but not too much: not more than the traffic will bear: indeed a good deal less so as to keep the traffic humming. In this as in so much else the conflict of Dominion and Province works our ruin: each wants its share and more.

It is commonly thought that the stimulus to mining described above would be lost under a return to the gold standard. This is absolutely not so. If we return to a gold dollar of 23.22 grains of fine gold we lose it: but at a lower gold content we keep it, or even improve it. We could add alloy to give the coins size. If we set the gold content at less than the paper value of gold, there would be a stimulus to mining that would last for years: as it ran out we could lower the content again: this is easily done, this occasional shift of content of the coin, but using "gold certificates" for circulation and keeping the actual coin or gold piled up: redemption is actual and immediate but the amount of gold actually paid can vary.

This is as much stimulus as the industry needs or ought to have: anything more spells ultimate ruin to gold mining. Paper dollars and sovereigns and francs and marks, *never redeemed*, cannot last. It is a wonder that they have lasted so long. England and France and the United States, etc., carry vast reserves of unused, unusable gold in vaults as a source of "credit". Its credit is getting to be much like that of Mumbo-Jumbo, the wooden idol of the African village. It is not what Mumbo-

Jumbo does. Mumbo-Jumbo sits still. It's the *idea* that surrounds him.

If it ever happens that a great nation that has no mines and a heap of gold, as France has, (over $4,000,000,000 in 1935) decides to sell the gold and do without it, to set up an "index standard" and a "managed currency", it is all over with gold.

Gold has hardly any utility value. The fact that about a quarter of the annual product in fine ounces is used in industry is mainly a consequence of its honour and glory. It glitters. Its real use is low,—false teeth, coffin handles and bank directors fees, etc. But engineers don't want it. Apart from glory, a gun-metal watch case is better than gold, a gold knife won't kill a pig, and a gold goblet is greasy beside a ten cent glass. Other things are not only "as good as gold", they are better.

When in the middle seventies the German Empire decided to demonetize silver, down it came with a run. So it may with gold. Ten years ago, with all the "stage coach" talk, it looked quite likely. Now it is all right at present, but something may happen,—must happen sooner or later,—unless gold is restored to use and redemption. And if it happens,—good-bye Pickle Crow. farewell Noranda,—the grass will grow in the streets of Johannesberg and the cows will pasture on the Rand.

Redemption used to be thought of as implying an unlimited "reserve", as meaning that it must never stop. Some ancient Victorian, in a bank crisis of the 1860's, once said that London was within "forty-eight hours of barter". The magnificent idiocy of the phrase was as imposing as magnificent idiocy is: it has come down to us. But the whole world has had now about ten years of barter (if non-gold payment means barter) and is still revolving. Redemption can be used even if at times it "empties" the till; even if the Treasury has to say "yes, we have no bananas". What we should do in Canada is to restore gold, at a low content level, open the mint at that, redeem our money in and out and when we have no gold left wait till more comes in. At the worst we are no worse off than today.

The claim that the gold standard under present conditions "clogs" can be met by the simpler rejoinder "let it clog".

But what is the use of arguing: Let's put on our leather suits and go aeroplaning for gold. We'll sell it somehow.

CHAPTER SEVEN

DEBIT AND CREDIT IN ALBERTA

Sunny Alberta and How It Went Broke—The
New Winds of Doctrine—Boom-Boom—
Legislating Prosperity—The Cup and the Lip—
Court Decisions as the Wicked Fairy—What the
Social Credit Movement Offered.

Sunny Alberta is a land of contrasts. In point
of altitude it begins at the summit of the Rocky
Mountains and ends at the bottom of the Saskatchewan. In temperature it will freeze you at
a few hours notice with forty below zero and then
wipe it all out with a Chinook wind and beg your
pardon for it. In point of latent resources, in and
under the soil,—coal, gas, metals,—there's literally no end of it. But for immediate resources, it,
the province, finds it a little hard to borrow
twenty-five cents.

The province consists of a stretch of territory
that descends from the eastern slope of the Rocky
Mountains out on to the great plain watered by
the Saskatchewan and the Peace. In area, a
quarter of a million square miles, it exceeds all
German-speaking Europe, Germany, Austria and
Switzerland,—and more than doubles the British
Isles. Its population of three-quarters of a million would just make one first class European
city.

The southern boundary of the province is the
line of the 49th parallel, separating Alberta from
the United States. Nor is the division purely

imaginary. The relatively infertility of the southern area, once labelled the Great Desert of the Saskatchewan, and the relative sparseness of the population, gives to the southern boundary something of reality; Alberta is not in the United States.

Eastward, beyond the 110th meridian begins the sister province of Saskatchewan, so akin in nearly every economic feature that to the outside world the two seem one. What one thinks today, the other thinks tomorrow. They share, among the Provinces of Canada, the distinction of being without a sea coast, land-locked, without maritime tradition or connection. Their "foreign policy" is limited to the question of American boot-leggers and Montana horse-thieves.

Alberta ends at the northern parallel of sixty degrees, beyond which begins the Northern Territory, still controlled by the Federal Government. But there are so few inhabitants that the division is of little account. In the south and centre of the province, where once were the "prairies" of the Great Plains, extends the grain country of the "wheat industry",—mechanized, rationalized, specialized, scornful of the old-time "farming". This is the country now humbled from pride to disaster. Further north is more varied country, rivers and hills, and on the great watershed of the Peace, (Alberta shares it with British Columbia),—one finds a wooded undulating landscape, such as Upper Canada once was, a country that in fancy seems the last hope of the sunset, still unspoiled by civilization.

The whole province seems more or less bedded on minerals and oil. No one yet knows how great may be the latent resources of Alberta, how usable the coal of its foothills, the natural gas of its valleys, the oil buried below its plains. But in the general sense there is no doubt of the vastness of its unused heritage. If the Social Credit theory is based on the collective rights of the people to their common heritage, it is well grounded in Alberta.

The climate of the province is humane. There is bitter cold, hard and piercing and dry, fit to split the thermometer, but it is tempered by the soft spring wind and the early rains that blow from beyond the mountains, and wipe away the snows with the April tears of repentence.

Till the Canadian Pacific woke the West from silence, Alberta was a part of the vast, romantic and unknown West. Lieutenant Butler (Sir William Butler) crossed it in 1871 as Mungo Park might have crossed Africa. Its emptiness was inconceivable. "One may wander," he wrote, "five hundred miles without seeing a human being or an animal larger than a wolf."

With the railway the West opened up. With the nineteenth century it opened wide up. Here was a country where agriculture moved on a chequerboard, where ten-horse teams hauled ten-furrowed plows in fields so big that they disappeared over the horizon; a country where wheat was threshed before it was even dry. "The Granary of the Empire, Free Homes for Millions, God

bless the Royal Family"—so ran the legend of the
Arch at the Diamond Jubilee of 1897. After the
turn of the century all the world poured in,—
Germans, Ukrainians, a polyglot multitude mixed
with an "American invasion" that moved from
the deserted farms of Kansas like Mormons on the
march. Even the Royal Family came. The
Prince of Wales took a ranch.

Thus grew Alberta, or rather thus was Alberta
raised like a circus tent in the shouting years before the War. Hand in hand with Saskatchewan
it became a province in 1905, and from then until
the Great War all was prosperity, advance, confidence with a braggart sense of unlimited great-
ness still to come. Even the War was expected to
be only an interruption. It was expected that
after Alberta had licked Germany the same pro-
cession of rushing immigration, roaring transport
and mechanized farming would go clattering fore-
ward. Indeed it tried to. For many years after
the war, the situation was full of hope and confidence. The census of 1921 showed a population
of 588,000 with two twin rising cities, Calgary
and Edmonton of about 60,000 each. The province shared to the full in the delusive hope of
Empire settlement, of tidal immigration, of an unlimited world market of wheat. The public debt
stood, in 1919, only at $34,000,000. Munici-
palities borrowed with ease in double-handfuls
and paid on the nail in gold in New York. But
with each successive year the clouds gathered. Immigration slackened and dried up at the source.

Without immigration the railways could not function. Empty town-sites with miles of new side-walks looked out over empty sidings and empty sheds. The frame was too big for the picture. It fell out.

Hence Alberta went broke about two years ago. The post war wheat boom had lifted it away up and the depression threw it down and broke it. The old political parties vanished. Even the "United Farmers" looked too old fashioned.

The total public debt of Alberta, just before the famous Social Credit election of August 22, 1935, stood at about $150,000,000: before the War (1910) it had stood at $14,000,000, and even after the War, as already said, at only $34,000,000, in 1919. The Provincial current deficit for the three months before the election was nearly $1,000,000. What had been rich farms and magnificent ranches were overwhelmed in mortgage debts. Prices for farm produce had fallen beyond belief. Five years of drought had withered the grain and dried up the water supply. The dust blew where once the grain had waved. The people were weary of depression, worn out with debt and wistful for prosperity.

It was then fully realized for the first time how one-sided is the economic structure of the West. In older Canada, the pioneer lived on his own: he settled depression with an axe, was his own butcher and baker and what he hadn't got he went without. His diversion was whiskey at 50 cents a gallon, and fighting in a tavern. As a motor car he had a buck-board and for a radio he talked to himself in the barnyard.   Economically, you might hit him hard, but you couldn't knock him out.   But in the new West all was different. Farming had run overwhelmingly to one special-ized industry, raising wheat on vast flat plains where machinery came into its own.   The farmer no longer fed himself, never saw a hen and had for his barnyard a corrugated iron grain elevator.

No wonder that new winds of doctrine blew over the empty prairie.   Theory lives best in a vacuum.   Hence the increasing vogue of all sort of new theories of money, credit and social recon-struction.   The doctrines of Major Douglas and others that filtered in under the name of "Social Credit" made an instant hit.   The word "credit" was enough by itself.

In moments of national emergency a prophet is always raised up.   In Alberta the provincial election of 1935 saw the raising up of a prophet whose name was William Aberhart and whose word was Social Credit and whose gospel a little handbook to be had at a cost of ten cents.

The Aberhart doctrine, or rather the doctrine of Social Credit in general, like all "people's doc-trines", has something in it.   It is based on the undeniable idea that no one of us brought any-thing into the world with us.   Each of us has his natural claim to a share.   We are, as it were, the joint heirs of a great estate, whereas our present social order dispossesses ninety-nine to instal one. We may imagine that, in a general way, of all the wealth produced in a year, a certain part is due to the original heritage, and each of us has the right to that whether we work or not. Rich or poor, wise or stupid, lazy or energetic—that much is ours. Call it, if you like, $25 a month.

The moment was specially fortunate for such a doctrine. The cry for people's money had led the Dominion Government to establish a central bank, the Bank of Canada, and the West had been disappointed with it. The Alberta farmer understood that the business of a central bank was to lend money to anybody who felt he needed it. When he saw that it did not do that, he looked for quicker action.

There is a charming little French story which tells of a little Parisian boy, smitten with fever and delirium, calling for Boom-Boom, a clown whom he had seen at the Winter Circus. In despair they buy him a toy clown. But he cries still, "That's not Boom-Boom". Then they get the real clown to come—the real clown in private life, a grave, dignified gentleman; and still the child calls, "That's not Boom-Boom". The clown, a true artist at heart, exclaims, "He's right!" and disappears and returns in his clown suit, his cap and tassels, his mouth painted to the size of a letter-box. The child claps his hands with joy and shouts "Boom-Boom" and is saved.

So with Alberta. Sick with adversity, feverish with anxiety, it called out for "people's money", for "cash-for-everybody", for "Boom-Boom" The Government of Canada fetched to the bedside the Central Bank. But the sick province took one look at the stately form of the Governor of the Bank and cried out "That's not Boom-Boom"! So then the election of 1935 brought Social Credit and the Rev. Mr. Aberhart, and the province resuced from its despair shouted "Boom-Boom, that's Boom-Boom"!

Mr. Aberhart's doctrine, in other words, was in its basis a theory of industrial society, such as philosophers have discussed ever since Plato.

But Mr. Aberhart had no intention of setting about his social credit attack with the slow approach, the sapping and mining, of the economic theorist. He proposed to use the axe. He proposed to swing it as did the famous Jack of the Beanstalk when he brought down the whole growth of the plant and with it the evil giant who had plagued his existence. Mr. Aberhart's "evil giant" was the Eastern Moneylender, and down he must come.

In other words he proposed to solve the insolvable problem of Alberta debt by hammering it out of existence; putting the axe to it: as Carrie Nation put the axe to the Kansas saloons and the English suffragettes to the House of Commons. It is what has come to be called "direct action" and it works like a charm.

The Alberta debt was a jigsaw puzzle that wouldn't fit. So Mr. Aberhart proposed to smash it. It was a contract that could not be paid, so Mr. Aberhart proposed to blot it out with tears: an oath that could not be kept: Mr. Aberhart would remove it with prayer.

Mr. Aberhart knew by instinct that the greatest ally that man can have is not physical power but the power of the spirit: the greatest force in politics is "religion", the super-self that ceases to reason and fights in ecstasy. It has been always so. Normans who prayed the night before Hastings defeated Saxons who drank. Mohammed conquered his world with the single sentence "Allah illa Allah,—God is great". Cromwell found that he must have men whose "hearts were in the cause", and he gathered his iron men with Bibles under their breast-plates.

So came forth Mr. Aberhart as to a crusade, denouncing the Money Power. "In Canada," he proclaimed, "money gets too much and man too little." It was like Mr. Bryan's America crucified on its cross of gold. Put it into simple language to mean that money borrowed at boom prices and paying its full interest in the pit of depression, no longer stands for a fair bargain,—and the idea is reasonable enough. Say it with prayers and it is overwhelming.

*   *   *   *   *

There were great expectations and grave forebodings on the triumphant election of the Social Credit. It is said that many of the plainer people in the towns called next morning for their "social dividend" of twenty-five dollars. As for Mr. Aberhart, he found himself in the typically British situation, as old as Queen Anne, of being suddenly changed from opposition to office and having to "make good". Fortunately there is also a British

precedent as to what to do, namely, to do nothing.
Mr. Aberhart announced that he must take "time
to think", a need he had never announced before.
He began to show a strong desire to consult people, to visit Father Couglin, his "opposite number" in the United States, to send over to England
for Major Douglas, the parent of Social Credit,
and to go to Ottawa, the Mecca of the provincial politician.   Meantime it was announced
that it would take at least eighteen months to get
the "social dividend" in working order.

*   *   *   *   *

The "eighteen months" of Mr. Aberhart,—a
phrase destined, I should think, to become
historic,—have come and gone this spring of 1937.
Mr. Aberhart has publicly announced the obvious
fact that he has not yet been able to initiate the
Social Credit system.   On this his political
enemies raised a shout that the thing was impossible and called on him to get out: and his political
supporters and various English advisers tell him
that the thing is easy, and shout to him to go on
with it.   Mr. Aberhart, knowing himself now to
be a *fact* and everybody else a *theory*, sits tight.
If we can't have Social Credit, he says in effect,—
let us have something else just as good.   His
peculiar "bulge" on the situation,—or is it "edge"
they call it,—is that there is no party anywhere, in
Alberta or near it, that would dare to propose to
put back Alberta debt where it was.

*   *   *   *   *

Meanwhile the moment is ripe for outside

people of fair mind to ask just what has been done during the Social Credit regime.   Of Social Credit itself there has been absolutely and literally nothing.   The Act put on the statute book under the name of an *"Act to Provide the People of Alberta with Additional Credit"* (September 1936) is only a sort of emergency loan act.   The registration (beginning August 10, 1936) of resident citizens entitled to the benefit of "dividends" was conditioned on the signing of a "covenant".   The pledges included "accepting Alberta credit and co-operating on production and prices", in other words "letting the government run a man's farm" and are not such as people on farms are apt to tolerate in North America.   The government is welcome to run the mortgage; not the farm.   So the pretentious "registration" and the "dividends" and the "covenant" have amounted to nothing and never will.   The credit statute can be used as an act for making approved loans,—as has been done elsewhere for nearly half a century under Allotment Acts, Land Purchasers Act and such.

With that has come the really large step,—chief sin or chief merit of the regime, as you like it,—of the legislative reduction of debt by forced conversion.   All the world knows in general terms what was done.   *The Provincial Securities Interest Act* (June 1, 1936) cut the interest on the public obligations of Alberta and obligations guaranteed by the province to a new schedule of interest running at about half of the contracted interest (4.89 per cent. to 2.50).

Moreover a *Municipal Securities Act* empowered all municipalities in the province to cut their interest to a flat 3 per cent. A few did; the larger ones not yet. *The Reduction and Settlement of Debt Act* (September 1936) provided that in the case of all "old debts" (those prior to July 1, 1932) all payments hitherto made as interest should count as a repayment of principal and the balance left, if any, be payable in instalments in ten years without further interest. On debts since July 1, 1932, the maximum interest was put at 5 per cent., and paid beyond that to count as repayment of principal.

Finally the government issued the *Alberta Prosperity Certificate,* a bright little imitation of paper money lacking only "legal tender", a body without a soul.

The Prosperity Certificate has now pretty will run its course, or at any rate its first course. Let us look back a minute,—before talking of the debt and see what happened to it.

The Alberta "Prosperity Certificates" were made up to look like "stage money", plentifully sprinkled with dollar marks and a framework of future dates on the back. They were issued by the Government and handed out as unemployment relief and in various other ways. In order to give them "velocity" in circulation they were made too hot to hold: the possessor must refresh them every Wednesday by gumming on its proper space a stamp that costs two per cent. of the certificate. They were not, and are not, "legal tender",

but the Government announced that it would redeem them at intervals for "all and sundry"—and
added "for good and sufficient reasons". As between citizens, anyone could, and can, take them
as a payment if he wishes. In many places the
first batch "sold" like hot cakes—as souvenirs.
After that circulation became restricted. The post
office (that is the Dominion Government) refused
them; so did all railroad, express, telegraph, insurance and similar companies. Theatres and
moving-picture houses did not take them. Country
storekeepers accepted them readily for purchases;
but they would accept a French assignat of 1789
or a George Washington continental dollar of
1778 rather than not make a sale. Nearly all big
stores refused them: the bigger the store, the firmer
the refusal. Companies of other provinces, unless
feverishly eager for business, refused them entirely,
or took only a percentage. But the unemployed,
not looking a gift certificate on the back, reached
out for them. Meanwhile the courts began "to
sit" on them. A court at Edmonton (open to
appeal) issued an injunction forbidding the city
to accept them from the province as its unemployment subsidy. The province replied with a
validating Act.

But the court never needs to pursue its pro-
cesses and appeals to the end, for the government,
having decided to redeem the certificates has cashed
in so many (viz. $295,791 out of $325,644, as
reported on Jan. 1, 1937) that the rest offer no
problem,—amounting only to $29,853. Proceeds

from stamp sales were $20,652. Finally, legislation of April 1937 ended their existence.

*   *   *   *   *

The public debt is a different matter of which the end is not yet, not by a long way. The Supreme Court of Alberta has declared, in two judgments of February 1937, that the province has no power to lower interest. The province answered with a "moratorium" and with a new statute of April 1937 cutting the principal of debts instead of the interest. This is just as easy to rule out. It is only a matter of words.

*   *   *   *   *

In summarizing and judging the existing situation, one may say, first, that in all these matters of the disputes, denunciations and recriminations of parties, it is better for us in Canada if we try to see not the harm but the good in one another: not to denounce but to comprehend. In every great movement that enlists the sympathy of thousands of disinterested persons there must be an element of right. So it must be, not with Social Credit, but with the Social Credit movement in the West. Social Credit in the sense of economic theory is mere wind, words and nothing else. It creates a vague ideal of "purchasing power" and wishes that everybody might have lots of it. So do I. I'd buy a new Fedora hat with it this morning. The demand that "purchasing power" must be given to the people means nothing more than that the people ought to be better off, and that society is all wrong till they are. All

sensible people think that.   But there is no way
to make an act of the legislature to sprinkle all the
people with "purchasing power" as you sprinkle
a lawn with a hose.

All that, I propose to examine in the next
chapter.   In that sense Social Credit is not only
dead but still-born: not only failed but never
started.

As to the Prosperity Certificates, the only advantage of their issue was that the expedient saved
for the time being that much additional borrowing.   The disadvantage is that the episode further
impaired Alberta credit and leaves the temptation
to make more issues.

The debt reduction acts must remain in sus-
pense until the Privy Council decides on them,—
in 1938 or later.   As is usual with decisions turning on the interpretation of economic and fiscal
powers under a federal constitution, the Court can
decide either way.   You can argue that the power
must belong only to the Dominion because the
Dominion has control of interest (B.N.A. Act
1867 (91)): or that it belongs to the province
because the province has sole control of "proper
and civil rights within the province" (same statute
(92)).   The one clause is misty in meaning: the
other is a dense fog.   You can grope as you like,
argue and choose as you want.   It's just like split-
ting a straw,—equally easy north and south or east
and west.   Anybody familiar with the American
cases, the Income Tax Case in Grover Cleveland's
time, the Insular Tax cases, the hundred and one

Interstate Commerce and Trust cases and now the
famous Gold Acts and the NRA and the other
cases,—knows how easily judges can disagree,
what mountains of argument can be piled up,
what years of delay may elapse over matters that
common sense could settle with a pen and ink in
five minutes.   Or compare, if one will, the recent
Privy Council decision invalidating the labour
and wages legislation of the Dominion Parliament
of 1935.   'Heads or tails' would do as well.

England fortunately is free from all this bug-
bear of the impediment of constitutional limita-
tions.   Every act of parliament is a good act.
They can vote social credit,—as far as *voting*
goes,—in a day.   The first need for social progress in America is to get rid of having the courts
interpret economic powers.   Indicate the field and
let the legislatures act: let the central one (Congress at Washington, our parliament at Ottawa)
take precedence when they clash.   If this is centralization,—as Patrick Henry said of treason,—make
the most of it.   The present method has no virtue
but delay: the legislatures in time can circumvent
it: Mr. Roosevelt, not being allowed to "restrict"
hogs under the AAA (ruled out by the Supreme
Court) now conserves them (keeps them unborn)
under the BBB.   The Supreme Court under such
a system merely turns into the Wicked Fairy forgotten at the christening of the Sleeping Beauty,
and emerging from the cupboard to distribute general damnation.

*   *   *   *   *

To kill Social Credit with a Privy Council decision makes a martyr of it.   The thing should be
decided not on the question of the competence of
a legislature but of the righteousness of a law.   If
it is right that Alberta debt should be cut and cancelled, then cut and cancelled it ought to be: all
the Privy Councils that were ever privy can't make
it otherwise.

Many people perhaps will think that if the debt
cancellation was wrong, then any way to get rid
of it is right.   If any stick is good enough to beat
a dog, let the *ultra vires* stick beat the Social Credit
dog.   Just as Mr. Roosevelt finding the *ultra vires*
declarations in their turn an obstruction is using
the senility stick to beat the *ultra vires* dog.

The whole system is wrong and works evil.
You can never persuade the people of Alberta to
abandon error by that means.   And moreover
there is this awkward feature about the situation.
If the Alberta acts are invalid then surely a large
part of the Saskatchewan debt reduction of 1936,
which removed $75,000,000 of debt, must be
invalid.   If a province cannot cancel a debt against
the consent of the debtor (the *Independent Order
of Foresters of Toronto vs. the Lethbridge Northern Irrigation District*), then that gives the same
right of protest to the individual debtor, even if a
majority have waived their claim.   In the case of a
collective mortgage (the thing commonly called a
bond) the terms of the document itself provide
for collective action.   The individual bondholder,
apart from fraud, must act with the others.   But

in the case of general farm mortgages, each one a transaction in itself, no amount of agreement among loan companies and mortgages, can constrain the creditor who does not consent. I am no Portia, but that seems to me sound law. Caveat Saskatchewan.

The truth is that this whole instrument of judicial decisions to settle the economic powers of the respective parts of a federal government is out of date. Federal government,—one of the greatest advances ever made by man in its political sense,—is out of harmony with the economic world of today. The present situation in Canada and in the United States has come as one of the unforseen consequences of federal government.

The conspicuous success of federal union in the definite formation of the American Republic in 1789 (a thing impossible without it), its application in Switzerland, in Germany, and presently in British North America, gave to federal government in the nineteenth century a singular prestige. Political philosophers such as Sidgwick, in terms of cold theory, and Tennyson, in the warmer language of poetry, could see foreshadowed in it the "parliament of man" and "the federation of the world". The peculiar weakness of federal government on the economic side passed unnoticed. The entire stress was laid on the possibility of political union for peace and war, where union under a single government was not yet possible. In any case the economic weakness did not exist in a group of scattered settlements without organic communication. But as these developed into a world of highways, canals, railroads, and telegraphs, and then as there began the epoch of the great corporations, of nation-wide business, of standardized products, and still more when electricity and power production and "radio" annihilated locality and space—federalism in the economic sense became first clumsy, then difficult, and now impossible.

The federated states of the modern world must unite, economically, or break. It is interesting to observe the varying fate that is overtaking them. The United States ultra-federal, i.e., over-separated, under the jealous "States rights" influence of the earlier life, became more and more united in actuality by the decisions of the Supreme Court from the days of Chief-Justice Marshall onwards. What the courts could not do was done by the sword of the Civil War, by amendments written in blood. After the war a progressive series of decisions kept reducing and avoiding federalism, kept extending national power over all the republic. The post-war development carried this process still further, and culminated in the Roosevelt programme of the NRA which passes the steamroller over the economic rights of the States and of the individual. In dissenting from the Gold Decisions of February 1935, an aged judge cried out, "The constitution is gone"! He was quite right. It is gone—just in time. It would have throttled the republic. The sheltering arm of federalism had changed in a hundred years to a suffocating clutch.

*   *   *   *   *

Social Credit then as theory is moonshine. Social Credit in its full legislative sense has not been enacted and is not likely to be.   Mr. Aberhart's statements, as from March 1st, seem to make that clear.   And the legislation actually put on the books by the Social Credit party has been brought to a full stop.

But the real achievement of Social Credit, I say it openly and fairly, lies elsewhere.   The Social Credit movement, more than any other factor, compelled all Canada to turn its mind to the debt question.   Government, and ours at Ottawa especially, for we live in peace, is apt to grow complacent in office: alternating from a decorous ministry to a decorous opposition, keeping the tariff, and the annual deficit, and the railway muddle as a joint heritage or stock-in-trade: soothing as best they may the sobs of the Maritimes, tabulating the weather, taking holidays at Geneva, and holding, every now and then, a Royal Commission on the Solar System.   Would that such halcyon days were forever possible!

From all this, "Social Credit" woke us up, as Thomas Jefferson said of the slavery question, "like a fire-bell in the night".   The election of 1935 swept the Province of Alberta cleaner than ever any province of the size was swept: or if this is not correct, it can't be far wrong: 56 out of 65 seats is pretty clean sweeping.

*   *   *   *   *

I found everywhere, even in the other provinces, a great deal of sympathy with the Social Credit movement, often in the most unlikely places. Retired colonels of Victoria, dozing off to sleep in the sunset: college students with nothing to lose and willing to repudiate everything: people tired of poverty, worn with hard times: young people full of hope, and old people filled with despair,—found in it a vague sort of gospel. I never met anybody who understood it. They expected *me* to do that because I was an economist. But the feeling that there "was something in it" was widely spread and deeply rooted.

It is impossible to foretell just what will be the final upshot of this legislative session at Edmonton. A section of the Social Credit party have attempted, not exactly to bolt, but to shove from behind. They want to make Mr. Aberhart "get a move on". They want him to bring in Social Credit, the real thing. They want to bring over an English expert and let him try. Mr. Aberhart won't move. "No living boy shall carry me," said Mr. Pickwick, and no living English expert can shove Mr. Aberhart.

Meantime half measures fail to soothe the rioters.

The Marketing Bill presented to the legislature in March 1937, will have no particular consequences. It empowers the executive government to buy Alberta produce and sell it in other provinces and abroad for "real money" and to buy outside and foreign goods and sell them in the province for Alberta credit. But this will not make the outsider (the word means a fellow Canadian) or the foreigner pay a penny more or take a cent less. It will merely interpose the added cost of delay and risk: Alberta goods will be swapped for outside goods just as they are now with the added friction of Alberta credit. Private sale cannot be prohibited (even provincial power must end somewhere) and the bill therefore will be ineffective as far as changing the social system is concerned.

The truth is that neither Mr. Aberhart nor any one else who might replace him can, or will, bring in "Social Credit" in the sense of a monthly cash dividend paid to each resident,—the plain, obvious sense of the original platform. Mr. Aberhart used this lever to turn out the old government: others may use it on him. But the lever once used is thrown away.

*   *   *   *   *

Up to the moment when this book is written, the spring session of the Alberta Legislature leaves Social Credit still suspended like Mohammed's coffin. The attempt of some of the party to bolt,—or rather to shove Mr. Aberhart from behind,—has not succeeded. That is apparently not the way to get at Mr. Aberhart. The new debt legislation, referred to above, cutting principal instead of interest, will get into the courts and stay there. A commission,—with power to hear, and even to think, and to go anywhere,—is to "organize Social Credit". In other words, is to do exactly what Mr. Aberhart has been wanting to do,—and can't do,—for two years. The Dominion, it now appears, has been advised not to lend money to the province.

What will happen is probably this. The sunshine will break out again over sunny Alberta. The wheat will wave and the price will jump. Of course the Dominion will lend money,—Ottawa was never cruel,—and anyway if it is true that the province doesn't need it, then they are just the people to lend it to. The Commission will report on Social Credit,—say half a million words. No one will read it because on the day it comes out there'll be a ball-game between Edmonton and Lethbridge, or a stampede at Calgary, or a three-headed calf born at Wetaskiwin and Social Credit will be off the front page.

CHAPTER EIGHT

THE PURE THEORY OF SOCIAL CREDIT

The Ancestors of Social Credit—Thorstein Veblen and Frederick Soddy—The Technocrats and Life by the Erg—Major C. H. Douglas—Banks and Bunk—The Social Heritage and Dividend—The A+B Theory.

Everywhere in the West I found what are called "thoughtful" people—it means people who can't think,—anxious to ask me whether "Social Credit" could really work and what was the "theory" of it. "Come", they said, "you are an economist; explain it to us."

But when I said, as economists always do,— "To understand Social Credit we must go back a century and a half," they said, "Let's keep it over till Friday."

So I never had a chance.

Now that it comes to cold print I get my opportunity.

I am quite convinced that Social Credit in its proper sense, with "dividends" and a "heritage" will never come into being in the West or anywhere else. Mr. Aberhart's "eighteen months" will be as slow in maturing as the Greek Kalends. At the same time it is altogether likely that a "Social Credit party" is here to stay, at least for some time. It will be a people's party of radical reform, having about as much to do with social credit as the Liberal party has to do with liberalism, or the Conservative party with conservatism.

135

This is always the way with parties. "Socialist parties" become bourgeois as they have in France, "labour parties" quit work and wear evening dress and "clerical parties" go to the devil.

But meantime each keeps a sort of tradition of its origin. So it will be with the "Social Crediters". They will preserve a imaginary background, a sort of sacred ideal which they are supposed to represent, too holy for current use. Thus in the South Sea Islands the natives have a god so exalted they must not even pronounce his real name. He's just called Oom. Social Credit is going to be the Oom of the Canadian West.

So it is proper to examine just what are the imaginary, ideal doctrines on which the party bases its existence. If they are once for all unattainable, like liberalism, it is just as well to know it.

*   *   *   *   *

Social Credit did not spring from the soil of the West. It blew in on the wind from outside, like the locust and the potato bug and the rust on the wheat. It traces its doctrines back to the books of certain well-known writers just as new families trace their descent from the Plantagenets.

Of these writers the first is Thorstein Veblen (1857-1929), author of the *Theory of the Leisure Class* (1899), *The Theory of Business Enterprise* (1904), *The Engineers and the Price System* (1921) etc. I knew Veblen well. He taught me at Chicago thirty-eight years ago when I was a graduate student in economics. Veblen had a beautiful and thoughtful mind, free from anger and dispute, and heedless of all money motive. As a lecturer he had no manner, but sat mumbling into his lap, scarcely intelligible. But the words which thus fell into his lap were priceless, and after all Malthus had a hare-lip, Demosthenes stuttered and Oliver Cromwell choked. The ideas of the lectures were gathered later into Veblen's books. The central point of his thought is that human industry is not carried on to satisfy human wants but in order to make money. The two motives do not work, thinks Veblen, to a single end as Adam Smith and John Stuart Mill had thought they do. They fall apart. Hence a lot of people get too much money. These have to find ways of spending it in "conspicuous consumption". This is the "leisure class", a sort of flower on a manure heap.

Contrasted with the "money makers" are the "engineers", that is men who make *things* not money,—the "real boys", so to speak. They could satisfy all our reasonable wants if they guided industrial society. But they don't. The money getters, with their leisure class women and their "honorific expenditure", have entrenched themselves as "Vested Interests",—and there you are! What did Veblen propose to do about it? Nothing, so far as I remember. They "let him out" of Chicago University: he taught in New York at the New School for Social Research from 1918 till his death in 1929. His writings, brilliant though they are, are too abstruse for popular reading, and not abstruse enough to be unintelligible and rank as gospel, like the Social Credit of Major Douglas.

Veblen's classes were small, only four or five of us. He used to lecture also on the Primitive Economics of the Navajo Indians. Why we needed to know about them I can't remember. Perhaps people distressed over the modern world turn to the forgotten quiet of primitive life, as moralists turn to the simple ecstasy of early christianity. The Navajo Indian class was very quiet. After a few minutes you could hear its deep breathing. I sat behind a pillar, the only one in the room. Veblen, not usually unfair, refused one man his "credit". He told me afterwards the man had slept in his class. I said I hadn't noticed it. Navajo is pronounced Navaho: I got that much out of it anyway.

With the name of Veblen goes the far more celebrated one of Frederick Soddy. Like Hamlet and Yorick, I knew him well. We began work together as junior lecturers at McGill in 1901. He was promoted to higher spheres, was taken and I was left. He was awarded the Nobel Prize in 1921, is now Professor of Chemistry at Oxford, and his name ranks second only to that of Lord Rutherford,—another McGill man,—among British physicists. The distinction about old McGill is the men who are not there.

Soddy, a physicist and a chemist, began writing economics on the side: in fact, he wrote one-sided economics and for that reason his writings caught on. His *Money Versus Man* (1931) went all over the West. Soddy, like Veblen, shows that science and machinery can easily supply all our wants. But the devil in *Money Versus Man* who spoils our paradise is not Veblen's capitalist but Soddy's Banker. This economic snake, by using his power to "create money" with a pen and ink, by making entries in a ledger,—in other words,—"coining credit",—this reptile steals our fortune as we make it: or, if you like, this skunk sucks society's eggs as she lays them. The invention of the cheque system, says Soddy, has "resulted in the banks, not indeed coining money as that is quite unnecessary, but creating money, without even the issue of printed notes, which they lend at interest to those who will pay interest on the pretended loan. . . . The issuer of money who first puts it into circulation cannot help getting something for nothing."

Soddy proposes to "make a total end of the system of fictitious credit". . . . "The replacement of national money of the two thousand or more million pounds sterling issued by the banks (Soddy presumably means issued in cheques) is is an act of tardy justice to the community."

If a banker is an honest man, up to your standard and mine, Soddy has much to answer for. If a banker is a social parasite, to be sprayed to death like a prairie potato bug, Soddy ought to have a statue.

I always feel that Soddy is quite mistaken in his view. Banking is an honest trade. It needs

regulating but so does every other.   Personally
I'd sit down and eat with a banker any time,—
even go into his house,—if he had any liquor in
it.

*   *   *   *   *

Then came the "technocrats" and for a moment
made a noise all over America.   When I was
lecturing in Alberta, an anonymous correspondent, anxious to insult me, sent me one of the little
manuals on Technocracy on which he had written, "Don't read this; you might learn something."   He was mistaken.   I had read it, and I
had learnt a lot.

"Technocracy", of which the valuable part is
now embedded in the Social Credit theory, contained a lot of truth; and what is more it taught
it to the world.   It "got over" to the public
things that plenty of inarticulate economists had
mumbled for fifty years.   It showed that our
enormous increase in machine power gives us the
means to satisfy, and oversatisfy our wants.   But
when the "technocrats" turned from destructive
criticism to the attempt to reconstruct society,
their ideas became ridiculous.   Their notion was
to replace money prices and wages by the measure
of the "ergs",—or units of physical energy,—
put forth in work.   One asks at once how many
"ergs" is a stenographer "erging" when she
pounds a typewriter: how many "ergs" does a
clergyman "erg" in the pulpit, a poet, how many!
and, most unhappily, an engineer?   But the vil-

lage blacksmith comes into his own: he's the real technocracy boy.

But at least the technocrats showed that we are now dealing with the Economics of abundance not of scarcity. Presently Mr. Stuart Chase said it in his own inimitable way, and all the world heard it. Our only problem left is what we are going to do about it. Neither Stuart Chase, nor anyone else, outside of Alberta, knows that yet.

*   *   *   *   *

But the principle, immediate source of the Alberta doctrine are the various books of Major C. H. Douglas, a Scottish engineer, dealing with *Credit and Democracy,—Economic Democracy, Social Credit,* the *Monopoly of Credit,* etc. The gist of these, and pamphlets of similar topics have been gathered into a single *Douglas Manual* which contains all that is necessary for salvation.

*   *   *   *   *

Major Douglas joins with Soddy in his views of banks and banking, and even dots the i's and crosses the t's of Soddy's academic phrases. "As the situation stands at present," he says, "the banker is in a unique position. He is probably the only known instance of the possibility of lending something without parting with anything, and making a profit on the transaction, obtaining in the first instance his commodity free." The best thing that Douglas can say for the banker is, "There is no suggestion that bankers, as *human beings,* are in the main actuated by any anti-social policy." No, the idea seems to be that the banker, as soon as he enters his office, ceases to be a human being and starts to growl. The interesting problem with Douglas is, why is a banker not worse? What holds him back? "It may be asked," he says, "why a bank only pays a dividend of 25 per cent. or so. The answer is simple. Their real earnings are measured by the control over industry which they acquire,—earnings so rapid that in a few years the control will be absolute if not checked. The amount distributed in dividends is, or could be, any desired dividend of "this capital control".

All of this anti-bank stuff seems to me as erroneous as it is harmful. But it makes a great appeal because it corresponds with what seems a queer phenomenon to everybody who borrows money from a bank and who is unable to trace further the economic meaning of what is happening. Apparently the banker is able *to create money with a pen and ink.* To make a loan he just writes an entry in a book. To make a payment from one customer to another he just makes a second entry. In other words he can make all the money he wants out of an ink bottle; spiders making thread aren't in it with him: he can "create credit": he almost qualifies, if Douglas and Soddy are right, for the first book of Genesis.

Elsewhere I have set the villain down in verse, thus:—

"He sits there in his tall silk hat,
A great big Ledger laid out flat,
A rounded Glass beside him set
With which to magnify a debt,
An Ink Eraser, short and stout
For rubbing a Deposit out,
Ink and a lovely 'Banker's' Pen
With which to write it in again.

Soddy, you guessed it when you said it !
Hush! Watch him now, He's 'coining Credit'.
He doesn't see us! Hold your Breath!
Look past his Arm and Underneath,—
See that last Flourish where he joined it,
The Thing is done! By George! He's coined it."

But does the banker really make money out of
nothing? When John Smith, anxious to buy
raw material for his business and to pay wages
"borrows $5,000", it is Smith, not the banker,
who gets the goods and the services: Smith, not the
banker, who sells the finished commodity to Jones:
and when Jones pays Smith with a cheque it is the
banker, not Jones, who has to make good the
cheque. When the transaction is all over what
does the banker get,—interest, that's all and he
deserves it just as much as Smith and Jones deserves a share (called profit) of the goods made by
the labour of their employees. Did they *make*
anything? Not a thing. They just sat there, on
whatever they sit on, in their glass offices and let
the men work. If you want to be a Marxian
Socialist, be one; but don't pick out the poor
banker and crucify him alone. Hang up all the
the rest of us, and yourself, too.

"But," says the Social Crediter, still perplexed,

"can't the government do what the banker does?"
Answer, no, it can't. It can, if you like, open a
credit house on Jasper Avenue, Edmonton (rent
to pay at once, notice) : it can give a civil servant
his month's pay in the form of a credit in a book,
and he can pay his grocer with a cheque on the
credit house and they are, all three laughing together! At first sight it looks great! How far
will it go? Next to nowhere. First, you can't
give him *all* his pay in credit. Some of it he'll
need for cash transactions. He can't carry his bank
round into the saloons when he buys a drink.
Some of it he'll need to make "outside" purchases
of goods from other provinces, and some, let us
hope, for investments in shares and stock of other
places. If he buys a share in a gold mine,—as he
will need to once if Soddy's right,—then he needs
cash. At first you would think that this only
means that he must have part of his pay in cash.
It means far more than that. It means that there
is a perpetual leak in the credit house. It's like a
barrel of beer with a hole in it.

More than that: even if you get the barrel full,
that's all it will hold. When the credit house has
made accounts enough to cover the level of transactions back and forward,—civil servant to
grocer, grocer to farmer for eggs, farmer to grocer
for tea, grocer and farmer for *taxes,*—you will
find there is just so much and that's all of it. You
see, the *taxes* coming in this way are just a back-
laugh on the government: just a "take-that-and-
you're-fooled." If the taxpayer pays, as I do

for my income tax, a real cheque on a real bank, the government gets something. . . . If it only gets a cheque on a Soddy-Douglas Credit Shop, it is merely being made to take its own medicine.

So much for passing cheques to and fro. Nothing in it: all the advantage wouldn't pay the cost and the stationery and the furnace and the char-woman and the teller's salary.

But what about making loans? Can it do that? Oh, indeed it can,—free loans like free lunch. It can lend comrade Smith,—who hasn't a nickel and hasn't worked since he was old enough to drink,—a thousand dollars a day. Who's to stop it? A real bank has to think, will Comrade pay it back? The Soddy-Douglas-House simply answers, what the hell if he doesn't? Fetch another cheque book.

Honestly, my Social Credit friends, your bank is off. I can sympathize with social help, social effort, social anything. But when it comes to a social destruction, I quit.

Pass on to the next item,—the famous "purchasing power" doctrine. Major Douglas has stated the basis of it with such exquisite accuracy; such scientific nicety,—that I can't understand a word of it. Here it is in the following passage under the name of the $A+B$ Theorem. I first read the passage years ago: have read it again and again since: I have, as the clergy like to put it when they get a call, prayed for light. I have never got any. I don't know, shall never know what it means.

THE A+B THEOREM

Rates of Flow of Prices and Purchasing Power.
(An Extract from "Credit Power and Democracy").

A factory or other productive organization has, beside its economic function as a producer of goods, a financial aspect—it may be regarded, on the one hand as a device for the distribution of purchasing-power to individuals through the media of wages, salaries, and dividends; and on the other hand as a manufactory of prices—financial values. From this viewpoint its payments may be divided into two groups:

Group A—All payments made to individuals (wages, salaries, and dividends).

Group B—All payments made to other organizations (raw materials, bank charges, and other external costs).

Now the rate of flow of purchasing power to individuals is represented by A, but since all payments go into prices, the rate of flow of prices cannot be less than A+B. The product of any factory may be considered as something which the public ought to be able to buy, although in many cases it is an intermediate product of no use to individuals but only to a subsequent manufacture; but since A will not purchase A+B, a proportion of the product at least equivalent to B must be distributed by a form of purchasing power which is not comprised in the descriptions grouped under A. It will be necessary at a later stage to show that this additional purchasing power is provided by loan credit (bank overdrafts) or export credit.

*   *   *   *   *

Based somehow on this is the idea of supplying "purchasing power" to the mass of the people. But what the people want is physical goods not bits of paper. Physical goods are only got by labour. The people, collectively, make them. Their 'wages' means the share they get in what is made. In other words, the true "social dividend" means work for all at good wages and agriculture for all at good prices. People can't eat paper.

Along with these arguments goes a muddy discussion, the 'just price' theory,—a problem as old as the middle ages. There is nothing new in the enquiry. It is only the solution that we want. Everybody who has even tried to study the political economy of our times knows,—everybody with a brain not ossified by wealth or deliberated by high birth,—that we live in an unjust world: that wages and salaries correspond neither to moral worth nor economic contribution: that free, utterly free, competition far from leading to social justice, favours the strong, oppresses the weak, creates the slums, submerges the labour class. It is only when the principle is held in check by the organization of labour, and by legislative interference through wages-laws, trust-laws, etc., that the wholesome basis of it,—every man for himself and his own,—can still animate society. What we need is not a new game but a new set of rules. Dimly they are taking shape. But all this lies outside of mere Alberta politics and Mr. Aberhart has no monopoly on human salvation.

Last remains the Social Heritage idea, the claim that we own the world in common, that we have all about us a world filled with accumulated contrivances and structures, altered and improved by labour, animated by ideas and operated by knowledge,—which is not the creation of the living, but of the past generations who built it up for us. Douglas speaks of the "social nature of the heritage of civilization". I fully agree with the idea. He cites with approval Thorstein Veblen's phrase "the progress of the industrial arts", as meaning something that we possess in common. "No one person," he says, "can have a monoply share in this: it is a legacy of countless numbers of men and women . . . a cultural legacy . . . . and the general community as a whole . . . . are its proper legatees."

This is a sound principle, a sound outlook on society. We already act on it to some extent in our new post-war application of 'relief' and the 'dole'. The Victorians let the poor starve and shed tears over their graves: we swear at them and feed them.

It is a point that would stand a lot of discussion. It would lead us to the interesting proposal for "free maintenance" as set forth by Bertrand Russell in his *Proposed Roads to Freedom* and by many others, including, in all modesty, myself. The general idea is that we might expand our present system of free meals for school children, free meals for people out of work, free meals for people in emergency distress,—into a general social institution of free meals for those who care to eat them. Imagine in your home town a bright, clean building, painted white, and inside it something as between a Rotary Club and a Ladies Church Social in full action. Eat there if you like, rich or poor, it's always there. After all people only eat three meals a day. They can't get away with more than their share without a stomach ache, and if you begin dimly to ge the idea of free clothes,— just plain suits,—one each,—well, you can soon dissolve all relief and public doles and all the rest of it into a sort of free community life as the basis of super-industry.

And the loafer? Let him loaf. If that's all he asks of life, his free meal and his burlap over-coat,—let him have it. He can sit and write poetry or play the banjo. We don't care. Mean-time the busy energetic clever people, thus set free, would be better off than ever.

CHAPTER NINE

MONARCHY IN THE WEST

I was in Saskatoon, Saskatchewan, when
Edward VIII, at 3 o'clock in the Saskatoon afternoon, December 11, 1936, broadcasted his abdication as King of Saskatchewan. I was in the
Bessborough Hotel. The clerk at the desk said,
"The King is to broadcast at three. That won't
interfere with you as you don't go on the air till
seven. You can hear him in the lounge."

There I heard him. There were just five or six
of us, strangers to one another and without talk.
We listened as did other groups all over the world,
to half a century of world history, going by in
nine minutes.

The abdication of Richard the Second in 1299
A.D. carried as its sequel and consequence a long
string of murders and executions that left a track
of blood over half a century of history. The
murders and executions were largely family affairs,
as between the royal family and the noble houses,
all closely related. First of all, the abdication of
the King was 'ratified' by murdering him. That
led to a protest from some of the relations and
friends and so the new King, Henry IV, executed
five of them the day after the protest. The Duke
of York, who had already murdered his brother,
the Duke of Gloucester, anxious to try to please

the new King, murdered his own brother-in-law, Lord Spencer, and sent his head on a pole as a present to Henry.   Henry was delighted with it. The executions went on and on, till the axe grew blunt.   The historians say that the "flower" of the nobility perished in the conflicts that followed. Those of us left are   just weeds.

Even when James the Second abdicated, or rather was informed that he had abdicated, things remained fairly lively for fifty-six years.   There were a couple of 'world-wars' (1692 and 1701), two Scottish rebellions and plenty of executions, including as the finale the beheading of Lord Lovat in the Tower (1747), the last beheading in England; the block and axe still kept in the Tower as an exhibit.

Abdication, as heard in Saskatchewan, was much quieter.   Apparently it was all over in nine minutes.   But it may be that the sequel is still to come.   At the moment there was nothing in particular.   The six strangers in the lounge got up and went away.   Round the town people listening in their offices said, "That's too bad, eh?" Just that, in most cases—"That's too bad, eh!" One man, indeed, told me that his stenogropher cried.   That's nothing.   They always do.   I heard one who cried when Governor Landon didn't get elected president.   Very likely one of them cried for Richard the Second.   Stenographers have to cry to show that they are still women.

But, mostly, people didn't say anything much about the abdication and mostly haven't yet.   The waiter at my dinner table said, "Too bad about the King, Sir! Table d'hôte? The gold-eyes are good." And the porter on the train that night said, "Too bad about the King, judge. Will I make it up now?"

The point is that the people,—the ex-King's subjects,—didn't know just how they felt, and don't know yet. Are their feelings just scratched, or are they stricken to the heart? Pain, it is said, lies chiefly on the surface. Men stricken with a deep, mortal wound often feel next to nothing, still walk and talk, and then fall down and die. It is perhaps something like that with us.

*   *   *   *   *

People who know nothing about it always imagine that the West of Canada is far less British than the East. Apart from the Maritime Provinces this is not so. It is even the reverse of truth. The West, as classified in our census into 'racial origins', has a weird look. But they don't act that way. They only ask to forget it. Even the high percentage of 'Americans' who moved over in the 'invasion' of 1905-14 makes no great difference as to the British connection and British institutions. Americans who were originally British, turn back again into British people. What do a few generations matter to a McGregor or a Howard or a Smith? And Americans who were not of British stock, but were German or Scandinavian or something else,—were never really Americans anyway, and can still turn into anything. A Scandinavian is an Anglo-Saxon already, one who missed coming with Hengist and Horsa. The truth is, though it is a mean thing to say, there is no such thing, racially, as an American, except an Indian: just as there is no such thing as a South African—except a black one: and no such thing, racially, as a Canadian. There is no American stock: 'stock' takes longer in the cooking than that. Hence, people of the second, and children now the third generation in the prairies, lapse back easily a generation or two, purged of American sin, and turn again to McKays and McGregors and Bakers and Smiths.

It used to be said that the last shot fired in defence of British institutions in America would be fired by a French-Canadian. It looks now as if there would be one more shot after his. It will be from the gun of an American whose name will be something like John Bull McGregor. His people will have been among the McGregors of Mississippi and the Bulls of the New York police: so he won't miss what he shoots at.

What is true of Americans is true, though in a lesser degree, of the numerous 'aliens', the European foreigners of the West. If one were to take mere tables of census statistics one could make out an apparently alarming case about the 'foreign' aspect of the prairie provinces. For example, The Bishop of London is reported to have implied just this kind of danger in speaking in the House of Lords (March 3, 1937) on the new Empire Settlement Bill. He said that a Canadian had told him that Canada needed 10,000,000 more British-

ers,—a sentiment as sound as it is true. He should
have made it 20,000,000. But he is reported to
have added that as things are now, the North-west
is in danger of becoming foreign. 'In Edmonton',
he said, 'thirty languages are spoken'. We might
answer so they are in London. The Bishop was
using a false argument in a good cause, a thing
that Bishops must often be tempted to do.

But a glance at the statistics involved will show
that apparently the agitation of the Bishop and
his friend is quite justified. Let us take the
'mother tongue' of the people of the West as
indicating their racial status: and include, in ac-
cordance with the official Canadian practice,
children of five years and under as speaking the
tongue of their parents.

In Manitoba, out of a total population (1931
census) of 700,139 there were 399,009 with English as their mother tongue and 42,499 with
French. There were 258,631 people whose
language was something else. Among these one
notices 57,312 of German language, 11,578 Ice-
landers, 31,758 Poles and 82,908 Ukrainians to
say nothing of 19,187 talking Yiddish. The
case at first sight looks pretty black, indeed as
black as the Black Sea. Contrast it with the status
of Prince Edward Island, where out of 88,038
Islanders, 86,463 have either English or French
as their mother tongue: where there is not a single
Ukrainian, only 1 Russian, not a damn Pole, and
just 1 Greek;—how he got in is not said. There's
a real country: only the trouble with it is that the

population decreases.   At least Ukrainians don't
do that.

Or take Saskatchewan.   It has 39 per cent. of
its people with an alien mother tongue.   Of its
921,785 inhabitants of 1931, no less than
138,499 were German in mother tongue (Mutter-
Sprache) and 70,545 Ukrainian: after which the
18,742 Poles and the 17,085 Russians seem a
matter of course.   As to the 78 Bulgarians we
wonder why they are so modest and don't catch
up to the 11,853 Hungarians.

Last comes Alberta.   Its total percentage is
not quite so high as that of Saskatchewan, but its
high enough, 33 per cent.   It has 461,713 speaking English.   In all these statements English includes what the Americans talk, which is just as
good anyway as what they speak in Clapham and
makes Somerset sound like a foreign language.
The Alberta French number only 28,145, with
63,410 Germans and 60,260 Ukrainians in a
total Slavonic group of 91,820.

*   *   *   *   *

The case of the French and the French language
in the West stands by itself and will draw from
many Canadians a sigh and a regret for the history
it represents.   The French were the discoverers of
the country.   Radisson and Groseillers were on
the Hudson Bay before the company,—indeed
they brought the company there—La Vérendrve
was on the plains (1731) half a century before
Alexander Mackenzie.   Even under the Hudson's
Bay Company the great majority of the 'white'

settlers were the Métis, French-Canadian half-breeds. The language of the West was French, with a top layer of Scotch. St. Boniface on the Red and Assiniboine was a settlement of over 800 French-speaking people when Winnipeg was only a straggling set of shacks, outside of Fort Garry, sheltering 241 inhabitants. The province at its inception in 1870 had 9,800 French half-breeds in a population of 12,000. Early Manitoba was bi-lingual. Its parliament that first sat in Mr. Bannatyne's house spoke and printed both languages. Its schools were French and English. If the star of the Empire glittered in the West for the English, the Church of the fathers was already there for the French.

From this joint heritage the course of history dispossessed them. The flood of Ontario settlers broke in on them. The Americans invaded them. Last of all, polyglot Europe washed over them,— much of it not even washed. Can one wonder that the French feel, one must not say a bitterness, but a wistful regret for their lost North West. And suppose we had had it and shared it on equal terms, with a bi-lingual culture to match the older East, it might seem perhaps a more balanced Canada, a more real unity.

It is strange what a queer touchiness surrounds the whole question of bi-lingualism in Canada. It shows how easily decent people can dispute among themselves over nothing. In the early spring of the present year quite a storm arose in the Canadian tea-cup when the gallant and distinguished English-Canadian at the head of our Broadcast Corporation, expressed his warm appreciation of our dual heritage and used the wrong phrase to express it.   The Ontario members of parliament understood him to mean that he was going to teach them to speak French.   The Leader of the Opposition quite rightly protested that he couldn't do it.   I know he was right because there are members now in the House to whom I tried to teach French at Upper Canada College forty years ago, and who can't speak it yet.

French vanishes as one goes west.   Winnipeg still has beside it St. Boniface with a French population of over 9,000.   Even in Saskatchewan there are over 42,000 French.   But in Alberta only 28,000.   In British Columbia there are only 7,768 and by the time you get to Victoria, B.C., they can't even pronounce "Parlez-vous Français."

But the French increase and multiply.   Their day may be coming.   A distinguished Scottish-French Canadian of Montreal told a Vancouver Lunch Club a few years ago that if immigration remained blocked the French would come into their own.   They would have their *revanche du berceau*.   When I was in Vancouver the Club asked me what it meant, and whether Mayor McGeer would give it to them.

The language situation in the West is reflected, again on the surface and only on the surface, in its newspapers.   The publication of foreign language newspapers in the Prairie Provinces of Canada has, so far as I know, no parallel in the world.   The only thing one could compare it to would be a cocktail party of the League of Nations at Geneva.

Most of the papers, for obvious reasons, are published in Winnipeg: but the circulation reaches out over the plains. There are listed in Winnipeg as weekly papers the Swedish *Tidningen, Posten*, the *Icelandic Lögberg*, and *Heimskringia Sameiningin*, and with these the *Czas*, which is Polish and means the *Times* and also the Polish *Gazeta Katolicka* (I think that must mean *Catholic Gazette*) and in German, the *Christlicher Jugendfreund*, the *Mennonitische Rundschau*, and the *Nordwesten*, the Danish *Church and Home*, the *Magyar Kanadai Ujsag*, the Norwegian *Narrona* together with quite a string of Ukrainian papers, the *Ranok* and others whose titles translated mean, the *Canadian Farmer, The Farmer's Life*, the *Herald*, the *Voice* and the *Workingwoman* and *Militant Youth*. If there is anything the Ukrainians have forgotten they can start another weekly and call it that. End up the list with the Yiddish *Israelite Press* and Jewish *Post* and you have a pretty varied lot, in all, counting a German paper of Steinbach, Manitoba, 22 weekly papers in languages other than English or French. Add to these the foreign weeklies published in Saskatchewan,—four German and one Ukrainian, and in Alberta,—one Ukrainian and one Danish,—and one has a formidable and interesting list. It is calculated at first sight to make the Bishop of London seem entirely right and to lead us to cable for his 10,000,000 Britishers at once. Some of

these papers moreover have a considerable circulation,—the Winnipeg Swedish *Tidningen* is put at
7,600, the Norwegian *Narrona* at the same figure,
the Polish *Gazette* at 7,000, the Regina German
Courier 6,500, and the Edmonton Ukrainian
News at 7,000. But these are the larger ones. The
circulation of the lesser ones is so small that they
blush to mention it and leave it blank.

But all of this, I repeat, is a surface phenomenon
quite misleading as to the present government and
future life of our country. The last thing these
foreigners want to do is to go back home. They
all want their children to learn English and to be
English-Canadians. They welcome every opportunity to have it so. Apart from odd communists
or revolutionaries they value our institutions. Of
republicanism they have no trace. Their foreign
papers and a few such things as Choral Societies,
or Beer Gardens, are just a gesture, a wistful regret, a tribute to their former mother country.
As it is they all want to learn to play hockey, to
attend high-school and college, to join the Rotary
Club, make money and move right up into golf
and bridge and have their wives members of the
Ladies Every-Other-Wednesday Culture Group.
In other words they want to be like us. Can you
blame them? Leave them alone and pretty soon
the Ukrainians will think they won the battle of
Trafalgar: and if the President of the Rotary
Club is a Bulgarian all he will ask is to forget it.

Take the case of the children of 5 years and
under. Statistically they would number in Mani-

toba about 90,000, in Saskatchewan 140,000, in
Alberta 100,000.   Of these the larger half can't
speak at all except to say 'pop' and 'mumm' which
is good Ukrainian.   In five years English will be
native to them.   In twenty years their mother
tongue will be gone.

It is well known how the European languages,
apart from English and French, wash out in
America.   Millions of Germans lost their mother
tongue in a generation.   I remember that when I
lived as a student in Chicago forty years ago there
were supposed to be in that city over 700,000 Germans and near-Germans, yet you'd look in vain
for anyone selling a German newspaper on the
street.   I roomed for a little while with a German
family.   The old people had come as old people
from Germany.   They had little English.   Their
grown up sons and daughters spoke English only,
even at home with one another.   The grand-
children knew no German and were learning it in
high-school.   Thus it will be with the Canadian
Northwest, the foreign languages, even the "thirty
spoken in Edmonton" will all wash out.   The
ill-conceived Manitoba school law of 1897, as a
way of keeping French, permitted any and every
language in schools.   That's all gone now.

*   *   *   *   *

The foreign languages, I am told, are but little
used, and are less and less used, in any public way
on the plains.   It is true that certain Mennonite
congregations still read their Lutheran Bible and
German service in their churches.   But that is

rather by conservatism of religion than of language. The same people would all use English at a political meeting.

English is indeed everywhere the language of politics. I can cite from direct knowledge the case of the constituency of a young and rising member of the legislature of Saskatchewan. The northwest part of it is overwhelmingly German in origin. There is a large section of 'Americans' in the centre, a heavy leaven of Ontario Scotsmen and a sweetening of Quebec French in the southeast. The rising young member is himself of Irish-Catholic-Canadian stock. Yet the language question never disturbs either political affiliation or personal contact. Human intercourse in the west is free and informal. Surnames are little used. Everybody is Dick, Bill and Fritz and Olie, and so everybody seems to come from everywhere.

*   *   *   *   *

In this discussion I leave out of count a few undigested and undigestible lumps of foreign nationality. Such are the Doukhobors, of whom we imported some 8,000 in 1901, increased to 14,000 in 1931. These people keep their own triumphant individuality. They believe in early Christian community of goods, think machinery wicked, go out hunting for Christ on the Prairie, like King Arthur's Knights and the Holy Grail. and take a run in their shirt tail as a protest against textiles. Their standard is too high for us. It is a pity they ever took a fancy to us. We

can't live up to them.   But in the broad aspect of
our future they count for nothing.

                    *   *   *   *   *

None of the public institutions of the West are
taken from those of these foreign peoples: none of
its laws: nothing of its basic ideas.

The Western landholding system is more English than what they have in England now.   It is
based on the holding of the yeoman farmer, working his own land.   In England, the yeoman, was
dispossessed in favour of a landlord class with
tenants.   But the yeoman had been transplanted
to New England—to Virginia and from there
under the name of a "loyalist" to Upper Canada,
and from there as a "homesteader" to the plains.
He doesn't know it but he's an Anglo Saxon
"thane" and beside him an English Norman Earl
living on a rent roll is a thing of yesterday.

The West took its school system from Ontario,
and its college system mainly from Scotland, via
McGill, Queen's and Toronto.   The short session,
the boarding-house student, the class-room lecture
in place of the tutor,—all that is Glasgow and
Edinburgh, not Oxford,—and certainly not the
Ukraine.   The churches, the public buildings, the
Queen's Birthday, all that is England or England
via America.   The government and its parties,
liberalism and conservatism, all that was British
till the United Farmers' idea came from the States,
and Social Credit from Scotland.

Who govern the West?   Look down the list
of the 65 members of the Alberta Legislative As-

sembly, elected in 1935; the names are practically all British. They are quite as much British as the list of the British House of Commons. Lack of space prevents proof. Any one interested may consult the list in the *Canadian Parliamentary Guide*, or the *Canadian Almanac* and that in *Whitaker's Almanac*. The same is true of Saskatchewan, with an odd German name or two. The Manitoba legislature elected in 1932 is almost all British in name, except for a Mr. Hryhorczuk, who would feel lonely, except for Mr. Bachynsky. But suppose that a quarter of a million Scotchman had migrated to the Ukraine. Half of the legislature by this time would be called "Mac": and the whole of the Cabinet.

Last of all one reverts to the "Americans' of whom we are told the West received a migration as between 1910 and 1914 alone of over 600,000. They brought with them, their own money and goods, and in money invested by and through and for them about $600,000,000. This was a calculation of our own government.

Did they Americanize, will they Americanize the West? They didn't and they won't. The West is more physically and socially separated from the United States than Eastern Canada. By an odd chance the forty-ninth parallel, an astronomical line, turned out to *mean* something. From Lake Superior to Manitoba the physical separation of the two countries is very real. Manitoba itself is an exception as the valley of the Red River presents a single and unified geography that

makes Manitoba and Minnesota one. If steamboat days had lasted one could have imagined a
dense, intermingled settlement making the two
countries indistinguishable. The railway connection of East and West stopped it in time. But even
now Manitoba connects more closely with the
south than anything a long way east or west of it
does. Seven railway lines and branches cross the
frontier north and south. Even at that, Winnipeg and St. Paul are at arm's length of 464 miles
by rail, and the border towns and villages,
Emerson—Pembina—amount to a little less than
1,000 people each.

For Saskatchewan and Alberta it is all different. The forty-ninth parallel marks fairly
well the division of the water shed. The little
streams that make the Missouri rise in Canada and
of the little streams that go to make the South
Saskatchewan the most distant tributaries rise in
Montana. But the steamboat never knew anything of such waters either way.

The land along the border happens to be in
great part arid and waterless. Old maps mark
it as the desert of the Saskatchewan. From Portal
(Saskatchewan) where the railway crosses as it
slants from St. Paul to head for Vancouver, to
Coutts, Alberta, below Lethbridge is a stretch of
about 400 miles uncrossed by rail. Then comes
the great barrier of the Rockies till it finally ends—
to leave a coastal strip where Vancouver sits close
to Seattle. Barring that connection there is little
back and forward intercourse or give and take and

the border is thinly settled. Along the south of Saskatchewan within forty miles of the border there are no towns of importance, except Estevan with a population of 3,000. The whole population (36 miles high) along the frontier of Saskatchewan is less than 60,000. Contrast this with Ontario where at the least 2,000,000 people live within forty miles either of the frontier itself or of the international navigable water of easy transit. On the American side of the line North Dakota, and still more, Montana, are but little settled along the border between the Missouri River and the parallel. The idea of people at a distance that the Canadian Northwest and the American Northwest are all intertangled has no foundation in fact.

If you want to see the real Canadian-American frontier you must go, not to the forty-ninth parallel, but to the Niagara-Buffalo boundary,— Go in summertime, round the first of July or the fourth,—they hardly know which is which. Go on a holiday and see the Stars and Stripes and the Union Jack all mixed up together and the tourists pouring back and forward over the International Bridge: immigration men trying in vain to sort them out: Niagara mingling its American and Canadian waters and its honeymoon couples, Canadians buying curios in the States and Americans buying querrios in Canada,— and such a chattering and fraternisation that it is no wonder that foreigners can't tell which is which of us. Or go to the Detroit-

Windsor frontier and move back and forward with the flood of commuters, of Americans
sampling beer in Windsor and Canadians sampling
lager in Detroit: there you don't really cross the
frontier at all, you drive under it in a tunnel. Or
come down here to Montreal and meet the Dart-
mouth boys playing hockey: or take the Eastern
Townships of Quebec where Lake Memphre-
magog refuses to recognize any separation, and
people out bass fishing hook up the international
boundary; or go to a "Ball-game" of the International League and sit in your shirt-sleeves and
root and try to remember which is your nationality.

Americans! Why, compared to us in the "east"
the western people of Canada never see them,
never hear of them. I'll make a slight exception
of the Lethbridge area, and Vancouver-Seattle and
the Red River, elsewhere the two are separate.

But after all what does the "Americanization"
talk amount to? Every now and then—and again
quite recently—English newspapers break out into
a discussion of what is called the "Americanization of Canada." The basis of the discussion
is always a sort of underlying fear that Canada is
getting a little too close to the United States. It
is the same sort of apprehension as is felt on a
respectable farm when the daughter of the family
is going out too much with the hired man. The
idea is that you can't tell what might happen.

In the case of Canada, the danger symptoms of
what may happen are supposed to be that Canada

is flooded' with American newspapers and maga-
zines; that Canada is 'deluged' with American
broadcasts, 'saturated' with American tourists, and
'permeated' with American ideas; that American
tourists cross the border in an unending stream,
and Canadian tourists go back with them like a
receding tide; that conventions and reunions as-
semble indifferently on either side of the line; that
education is almost indistinguishable as carried
on at Harvard or at Toronto.   All these things,
and a hundred more, are produced as a terrible
warning of what may follow next——the hand-
writing on the wall that signifies that our Bel-
shazzar's Feast of Friendship is nearly at an end.
In other words, a relationship which should stand
as a bright and conspicuous example for less
fortunate nations, as an ideal and hope for dis-
tracted Europe, is turned against us as a mark of
under-patriotism and lack of national spirit.

To my mind, the situation is exactly the other
way.   If Canada is being Americanized then what
England needs is to be Frenchified, and what
France needs is to be Anglicized——and both of
them to be Germanized.   If then one might take
the resulting amalgamation and Italianize it a
little, and even give it a touch of Czechoslovak
shellac rubbed on with a piece of old Russian
Soviet, the world would be on the way to peace on
earth.   That is to say, the best hope for the
European countries is to get into the kind of
mutual relationship now fortunately held between
the United States and Canada.

That this relationship is likely to end in, or even move towards, a political union, is just a forgotten dream. For those of us who best know this North American continent, on both sides of the line, know also that there is not on the present horizon, nor in the furthest vision possible, any prospect of a political amalgamation of the two countries.

The truth is that what we have in Canada and the United States is what all the world must get or perish. It is universal peace or nothing. Machinery prohibits war. Out of war, courage is vanishing as its supreme asset; personal size and physical power went long ago; soon there will be nothing left but machine equipment. Have it, and you win. Lack it and you lose. For proof, look at any of the recent pictures of the effects of Italian gas. I would like to inscribe a monument with the picture of one of those torn bodies on the burnt heath of Ethiopia, "The Death of Courage". It is not a triumph of civilization over savagery. It is a triumph of machinery over both. Our turn is next.

The union of the world can never be brought about by treaties, sanctions and the *ultima ratio* of war. All that, in the words of Tacitus, can make a desert but not peace. World solidarity can only come through unity of ideals, of interest, of understanding.

In past history, association and union did not go very far. They were blocked by all kinds of hindrances—physical, geographical, personal,

spiteful.   But they didn't need to go far.   Distance
did the rest.   Men out of arm's reach could not
hurt one another.   A little nation in a valley sat
snug: a people in an island lived in peace; a castle
gathered in its brood like chickens.

All this is gone.   An island is nothing.   A
valley is a grave,——as in Ethiopia.   Men must
unite or die: and for their union a written compact
is nothing but a rope of sand.   The only hope lies
in what would be academically called "the inter-
permeation of culture."   In other words, nations
have got to know one another.

Now the Canadians and the Americans know
one another.   That places the Canadians as a sort
of half-way element between the Americans and
the British people—creates as it were the nucleus
of a world union: not in the sense of an alliance
to challenge and menace the world, but as a first
area of solidarity from which it may spread
abroad.   If we could only send over to Europe a
few of our students to play hockey, or some of our
international crooks, the union might start and
spread at any time.

CHAPTER TEN

BRITISH COLUMBIA: EMPIRE PROVINCE

British Columbia: a Vast Pacific Empire Beside
the Sea—Vancouver, A Wonder City—The
"Pan-handle" of Alaska—Vancouver, the
Terminus of the Panama Route—Wheat Outlet—British Columbian Potential Population
35,000,000.

You cross the Rocky Mountains from the
prairies to British Columbia, and you are in a different place: you are in another country. I don't
know how to say it strongly enough. Let me
begin again. The Prairie Provinces are one place
and British Columbia is another. Many people
had tried to tell me this but they never succeeded.
I don't know of any words,—even of mine let
alone their poor attempts,—to express the fact.

British Columbia is a thing by itself: a vast
Pacific Empire beside the sea. It is only the fact
that it is as far from Europe as you can get that
so long kept it out of history. The ancient world
lived round the Mediterranean Sea. The British
Isles were away out in the dark. They called
them dimly the Tin Islands: the North Sea
coast was Ultima Thule: the Atlantic Ocean was
just a great black cloud, beyond which was terror.
In the course of twenty centuries the world shifted
its base. It centres now round the Atlantic Ocean
and the North Sea. The Mediterranean is just a
passage way,—drafty with high explosives, an
area for the next war. One side is sand: the other

ranges and history. At one end is a fight
lish Kilkenny cats—at the other, Turks.
is the real world. The real world lies
the Atlantic.

one would say that the Pacific Ocean will
displace the Atlantic. We, now living, can't
imagine it. But it will go a long way to supplement and rival it. And as it does so, British
Columbia will rise into splendour.

This absolute physical, geographic and climate
separation from Canada is of course more marked,
more cruelly emphasized in winter. As the early
evening is closing in your train is still on the flat
prairies. Everything about it is desolate, windswept with snow driven in fierce gusts. Even in
the lighted towns and in stations life is frozen
numb. Outside is the dark and the storm. Next
morning you are among the great gorges of the
Rockies, heavy with evergreen trees enbedded in
snow. There is deep silence. The cold has fallen
soft. It is like sleep. And from that, down
through the hills, the rushing streams and lakes
that lie open and unfrozen in the snow, snow that
diminishes and disappears,—and at the end the
sea, the open sea, and the sunshine on the harbour
of Vancouver and the snow-capped mountains
beyond.

Here is a city indeed, busy and bright with a
"shopping district",—(they don't call it "business section"; they're English) as crowded and as
crooked as Regent Street or the Rue de la Paix: a
harbour crowded with ships, literally, from all the

world, a harbour that never sees ice-breakers: as busy in January as July: at the sea end of it a vast park with towering trees as old as Genesis: beyond it great mountains capped with snow to recall Scotland, and over it is the soft wet air, salt with the sea, to call up visions of England.

Vancouver is a wonder city. There will be a million people in it in twenty years. It has the combined excellence of nature's gift and man's handiwork. God did a lot for Montreal, but man didn't add to it. Quebec is historical and has a majesty of situation, but a lot of it is squalid: Toronto,—I come from there myself, so I have the right to insult it,—Toronto is a village and always will be, if it spreads out a hundred miles wide: the prairie cities are impressive in their isolation and extension—fill in houses and they will be wonderful—but Vancouver is wonderful right now.

When I arrived in Vancouver, I said to the Press: "I am fascinated with it. You may have heard of O'Rourke, the Irish immigrant who went before a New York state judge to see about getting a vote.

"Have you read the Constitution of the United States?" asked the judge.

"I'm delighted with it," answered O'Rourke.

You see, O'Rourke didn't pretend to understand the constitution as yet, but he was delighted with it at the start.

That was me with British Columbia.

I looked at the fertile valleys and compared

them with my own poor little holding on the Old
Brewery Bay, Ontario, and my heart sank. Be-
sides this, my place seems as rugged as Scotland.
I'll have to turn it into a distillery.

They asked me later on at the Canadian Club
why I had never visited the province before. I
answered that, like so many other people, I had
never come to it because I didn't realize how
wonderful it was.

"If I had known what it was like," I said, "I
wouldn't have been content with a mere visit.
I'd have been born here."

*   *   *   *   *

Now let me start to prove what I say.

To understand British Columbia you must first
get an elementary grip on its geography, which
few of us outsiders ever do. When nature made
our North American continent, the west side of it
whether, as used to be thought, from shrinking as
it cooled down, or perhaps, as is now suggested,
from sliding sideways, was squeezed and furrowed
into great ridges like the fingers of a hand laid
flat. There they lie, the mountains of British
Columbia,—the Rocky Mountains in the world-
wide sense, or in the intimate geography of Canada, the successive ranges that lie side by side, the
Rockies, the Selkirk and the Coast mountains.
Here and there the ranges fall apart with wide
valleys and lakes opening in between, and in the
north they sink down to lower rolling land.
Through these mountain walls the heavy rains
from the great rain-clouds of the Pacific gathered

in streams and rivers and drove north and south
to find a way back to the sea.   In the north, the
Finlay and the Parsnip, joining to form the Peace
River, burst eastward through the Rockies, to find
themselves caught in the Mackenzie Basin and
diverted to the Arctic Sea.   Further north, on the
confines of the province, in country still scarcely
known, the Liard follows a similar course.   The
Fraser, moving north behind the Rockies, finds its
way blocked, is turned south and drives a deep
furrow of valley and canyon through the heart of
British Columbia, to reach the sea close to the
American border.   The most westerly of these
alternating belts of river and mountain chain,
is seen in the Vancouver mountains of Vancouver
Island,—which come up from the ocean again as
the Queen Charlotte Islands,—and the narrow
waters of Johnstone Strait and Discovery Passage
which refused to remain a river and let in the sea.

Greatest of all the Columbia, moving north
from its Kootenay tributaries, is deflected in a
right-about turn and flows back south behind the
Rockies, to pass far below the forty-ninth parallel
and reach the sea in the wide and beautiful sweep
that encircles the larger half of the state of Washington.   This was nature's boundary for the
Empire Province.   We lost it, through no one's
fault or error, in the give-and-take of the Oregon
award of 1846.   That British diplomacy ever
sacrificed Canada, is a myth: that it often saved
it, is a fact.   But in 1783, when first the United
States obtained boundaries, the continent was so

vast, its features so unknown, the need of new land so little and the future so far away, that lines and parallels and watersheds were accepted with but little knowledge of what they would ultimately mean. So British Columbia lost the state of Washington and the United States lost British Columbia.

*　　*　　*　　*　　*

But the Columbia River does not represent the province's only boundary trouble. There is also, of course, the "pan-handle" of Alaska, the downward stretch of heavily indented coast (in all some 35,000 square miles) that reaches downward from the sixtieth parallel to latitude 54° 40′ and shuts off the northern half of British Columbia from the sea. All of this "ought" to belong to British Columbia: only it doesn't and never did.

It was of this territory, finally allotted to the United States by the Alaska Tribunal of 1903 that Sir Wilfred Laurier said that Canada had again been sacrificed on the altar of British diplomates. He spoke out of the fulness of indignation, not of knowledge. The case was as clear as day. The Russians had explored and settled and fished all this north Pacific coast. Alaska was called Russian America. The Czar of Russia made a treaty with England in 1825 which made latitude 54° 40′ the boundary. It gave Russia the land for ten marine leagues behind the coast. The purpose and meaning, the sole purpose and the only meaning, was to keep the coast and the fisheries for Russia. The coast was deeply indented.   There were no complete maps.   The boundary line was of course meant to follow the indentations and keep away from the sea.   Otherwise British vessels could run in and out at will and every Russian inlet would be a British harbour.   Both parties were completely satisfied.

In 1867 the Czar, Alexander II, as a gesture to show how big he was (*gave* Alaska to the United States for $7,200,000.   (The annual produce now is worth in fish alone $30,000,000; in minerals $20,000,000.)   The United States didn't want the "ice-box" but they took it and paid for it just to show that they were as big as the Czar.

They took the boundary with it.   The Klondike gold rush made it all look priceless.   Hence the dispute and the award.

But if I were British Columbia I'd buy back the Panhandle now while it is still possible; or at any rate buy all that is south of Juneau.   Let the Americans see that we're just as big as the Czar and themselves: we'll take anything we can get. The Americans in 1922 gave the Republic of Columbia $25,000,000 for their old Panama claim that wasn't really worth a button, just to wipe away their tears.   Let them wipe our's away too.

*   *   *   *   *

In point of climate British Columbia is an ideal home for the human race, not too cold, not too hot, not too wet, and not too dry,—except in the hotels, a thing that time may remedy.   The mean annual temperature of 40 degrees that skirts the bottom of British Columbia is that of Cornwall and Paris. There is a thermal line that on the Pacific slope of the provinces marks an average January temperature the same as that of Atlantic City.

Vancouver Island and Victoria, to which I pro-pose to devote the next chapter, live bathed in the winter sunshine. They think the mainland cloudy by comparison. Their people should recall Lon-don, where in the month of January 1936, the *whole month,* there was only a total of twenty-three hours of sunshine, and in the December previous seventeen and a half hours. The city of Vancouver at least had a lot more than that.

A recital of the physical resources and assets of British Columbia is impressive. The first is its marvellous climate and fertility given to it by the geography described above. The ocean currents from the Orient, the Kurosiwo, keep it warm: the ocean rain keeps it wet. The soil and atmosphere combined to give its vegetation a primeval vigour that rears great trees, the Douglas fir, 500 feet high and ten feet across, that were living as young trees when the Greeks built the Parthenon.

The province contains 372,000 square miles. It is announced that the Yukon territory (205 square miles) will be joined to British Columbia to make a total of 577 square miles and a province reaching from the Arctic Ocean to the American border. It is said that the 'population' may re-fuse their consent. The 'population' are so rare that there is only the fiftieth part of a human being to a square mile. Eighty-three of it are Eskimos. There are 1,543 who admit they are Indians. The whites numbered 2,602 in 1931. They are nearly all transients. In my opinion they "own" the Yukon about as much as I own the Island of Montreal.

Even without the Yukon, British Columbia, measured in Europe, is more than half as much again as Germany: it is as much as all Scandinavian Europe (Sweden, Norway, Denmark and Iceland) which contains 350,000 square miles, supports a population of over 12,000,000 and is not 'in it', square mile for square mile, with British Columbia. It is true a large section of the province is mountainous and when the mountains are steep enough must be deducted from agricultural use. But mountains carry minerals and timber, and the slopes where not too steep *add* to the surface, not subtract. Few people have probably thought of it but when you think of it you see it. The rolling land of Ontario and the hill sides of the vineyards of France carry more acres to a surveyor's square mile than the prairie of Saskatchewan. To be exact, land with a slope of four to ten (quite easy to plough, crosswise) adds about eight per cent.: a slope of two to ten adds about five per cent. On the other hand the steeper a mountain is the less room it takes: a precipice doesn't take any at all.

British Columbia has 22,000,000 acres of farm land, of which only one acre in ten is in present use. Its forest area covers 240,000 square miles.

Of this 142,000 square miles is merchantable, 16,000 square miles is set apart as forest reserve: only 18,000 square miles of lumber has yet passed out of public possession.

The water power of British Columbia, reckoned at ordinary six months flow, is over 5,000,000 horse power: only 718,000 is as yet under installation.

The actual coal reserve of the province has been estimated as well over 20,000,000 thousands of tons. The Pacific coast fisheries of British Columbia produce two fifths of the fish output of all Canada. The salmon fisheries of the estuaries of the Fraser and now especially of the more northern rivers, the Skeena and the Nass are unrivalled. The development of whale and herring fishing at the Queen Charlotte Islands is a new feature. Figures of output and value show that the British Columbia fisheries have at times exceeded 20 millions of dollars. But these figures only tell a part of the tale. The province has 7,000 miles of sea coast. There are as good fish in the sea as ever came out of it.

All these figures mean that what British Columbia needs is people, more people, and still more. Land, labour and capital represented the triology of the older economists. The land (resources) is there: bring in the labour: the capital follows it.

Especially is this true because of the new Pacific orientation of British Columbia. It is no longer the *end* of America: it is the beginning of the

Pacific: and in a sense a point on the great circle that now swings round the northern continent via Panama.

Everybody knows of course that Vancouver took its rise as the ready-made terminus of the Canadian Pacific, the port of departure for the Orient and Australia. As that it rose from the surrounding woods of Burrard Inlet and flourished for thirty years. But the great factor in its growth now is the Panama Canal. Vancouver is now the Canadian terminus of the Panama route. Of its 4,000,000 tons of ocean shipping, as apart from the coastal and ferry trade, in and out, one half are to and from Panama. In 1935 imports and exports from Eastern Canada through the Panama were more than 75,000 tons.

The Panama Canal route is one of the great economic factors in the modern world and everybody in British Columbia, indeed in Canada, should 'get wise' about it. Its consequences have been utterly unexpected: and they are even now only beginning.

The Canal,—when the energetic Roosevelt the First drove the plan through and that grand old engineer, Colonel Goethals, constructed it,—was in reality a strategic, a naval idea. The Spanish American war of 1898 had shown the United States where they stood,—their navy in two separate compartments. The sensational voyage of the battleship Oregon, round the Horn, expressed it in capital letters. But the Americans hate 'strategy' as much as we do. So they called it a *commercial* canal: and the joke is it turned out to be one. Not that it makes enough money to pay interest on the half billion dollars that built it. But it readjusts, redirects, a vast quantity of the world's commerce, and none more than it does ours. It turns out that time doesn't matter for certain cargoes, notably for grain, which has got to wait for its market anyway. Hence the port of Vancouver ships out Canadian wheat for Europe at the rate of 40 to 70 million bushels a year. The highest point yet reached is the shipment of over 96 million bushels in 1928. Wheat for the Panama Canal route is shipped from points as far east of Vancouver as the eastern border of Saskatchewan. And the route is open all the year round.

Wheat likes to take its time: and so it appears do certain passengers. Already over 15 lines of steamers carry passengers on regular schedules from Vancouver to Europe via **Panama**. Most steamers take the trip in a leisurely way, the stops being part of the pleasure,—Hollywood being one of them. But the voyage in mileage from Vancouver to Southampton via the Panama is 8,500 miles, and the necessary time about 28 days. The voyage across Canada to Montreal and thence to England may be put (with the same class of steamer) at about eleven days. No one would 'hurry home' via Panama, as people use to in 1860. But many people are attracted by the trip. 'Cruising' has come as a new phase of the world's method of rest.

It by no means follows that the Panama Route will hurt our Canadian transcontinental railways. People will come via Panama to British Columbia for the cruise and return by rail,—people who otherwise would cruise somewhere else.

But even wheat and passengers are only the beginning of the subject.

The importance of the Panama route is such that public opinion in British Columbia should be directed in good time to the question of a second Isthmian canal. When it is built it should properly be a joint enterprise of Canada and the United States. At the present time the Panama Canal suffices, but with a much smaller margin than would be gathered from a superficial view of the traffic returns. In spacial capacity the dimensions of the Panama Canal are good enough. In point of length its locks can hold any ships in the world now afloat except the Normandie and the Queen Mary. In depth it is 41 feet at the shallowest. The canal is able to handle 17,000 ships a year. The highest annual traffic yet reached has been only 7,000 ships. Increasing the locks in size, it is said, can double the capacity, but there are obvious, general reasons for an international, rarther than a national canal.

In a financial sense there is still little temptation to build a second canal. The Panama cost $543,-000,000, the interest on which at 3 per cent. is $16,290,000. The canal made a return over operating cost in 1935 of $15,540,723: but if the interest is charged there is an annual deficit of

$771,618. But all this situation can change, if not in the twinkling of an eye, at any rate in the twinkling of a British Columbia Cabinet. If a new canal is needed there is the Nicaragua route, probably always the better one, but side tracked in favour of the present one. Advocates of the other route gave it a bad name and filled it with volcanoes which it hasn't got. The United States bought in 1916 for $3,000,000 from Nicaragua a monopoly right. But we could induce them to share it. The "Nicks" themselves are out of it. There is also the Columbian route below Panama, the subject, so it is said, of a lot of backstair's diplomacy. It is said that a British oil syndicate got a canal concession thrown in with the oil, but gave it back at the instance of the United States.

All of this the people in British Columbia ought to study. The first thing should be to get someone to make an address on it to the Women's Canadian Club. That has grown to be the way to start things in Canada. It's a pity there were no Women's Canadian Clubs back in past history. Columbus could have given a talk on "Where is the United States?" and saved years of exploration. The Renaissance could have been put over in one winter session.

I offered to speak to the Club in Vancouver on the "Prospect of a Second Isthmian Canal." They asked me what I knew of it and I said, "Nothing." That was why I wanted to talk about it. A person who knows nothing about a thing brings to it a freshness, of enthusiasm impossible

to those who know too much.   But the club decided against it.   They said it wasn't funny
enough.

But the great and outstanding aspect of the
empire province of British Columbia is its need
for further development, for more people.   Of
late years unfortunately a lot of people in Canada
have taken a bilious view of immigration.   The
French Canadians are against it: they think they
can attend to the increase of population right at
home.   And can you blame them unless the immigration was from France or Belgium.   Moreover what is now called 'labour' is against it.
Labour sees clearly, but it sees with only one eye
and can't see far.   Can you blame the people whom
we used boldly to call the 'working class' if they
can't look six months ahead.   We never gave them
a chance to.

Labour sees in the immigrant a man who has
come to steal his job at lower wages.   Foreshorten
the picture sufficiently and that is what you see.
How would we like it ourselves?   How would our
college professors like the import of Hindu teachers who could live on nuts and need only a loin-
cloth?   How would our bankers and financiers
appreciate the import of *real* cannibals from the
Marquesas?

But apart from French-Canadian and labour
opposition there is a new anti-immigration school
made up af academic socialists, pots without a lid,
the kind of people who call you and me the
'bourgeoisie', and use terms we don't understand,

such as 'social continuum' and 'sociological saturation',—which evidently means something they
wet. These people have invented for Canada the
idea of an 'optimum of population', and have put
it, for no particular reason at all, at 35,000,000
people.

The fundamental fallacy in all such thinking
is that the immigrant takes away the other man's
job. The truth is the other way. The tide of
immigration raises the home waters. The incoming immigrant, under proper circumstances,
attracts with him a great import of capital, of
physical goods and material, of intangible 'money'
to invest. He represents society 'moving house'
from one location to another. When you move
house you don't complain that there is no furni-
ture, you bring it with you.

For proof of this ask the Winnipeg of the
early eighties, when the hammers and saws were
noisy on Main and Portage all day and night.
People have told me of the big days of Regina
before the War, when it was changing from a
straggling town to a modern city, with the government buildings going up, with all incoming
trains full, and nowhere for anyone to sleep. In
fact they didn't sleep.

All these times can come again.

*   *   *   *   *

Now there is no doubt in my mind whatsoever
that British Columbia alone can support 35,-
000,000 people: not only can but *will*: not only

will, but will within the century. People alive now will be alive then.

Look at it this way. Population can be supported in either of two ways. People may live on an area, without any reference to its own fertility or resources by working up material brought in and taken out, or by performing services on the high seas and elsewhere and consuming goods sent in return. Thus might a community live and flourish on an ice-berg or on a rock. It is like taking in washing.

Thus live and flourish many of the millions that make up the 36 millions on the 50,000 square miles of England or of the 8 millions who live in the 11,700 square miles of Belgium.

But this is only for special areas. Obviously it can't be everywhere. But any place and every place, empty or partly empty, and with resources not used or not fully used, can take in people (under proper organization) up to the measure of its resources. Humanity lives from the ground under its feet.

Now take the magnificent resources of British Columbia as detailed above. Here are the 22,-000,000 acres of farm and garden land and the vast grazing country of the north. No market for grain, you say; can't sell fruit; grapes overproduced! All right, then take the almost unrivalled fisheries of the British Columbia coast, 7,000 miles long, is it not? No market for any more export of fish! you object. Catch one more salmon and you break the market? Very good, then let the people turn to lumber. We said of the forest wealth of British Columbia that it covers 142,000 square miles. Can't sell it? Too bad. But remember the enormous deposits of coal, the potential 40,000,000 thousands of tons. Or the mineral wealth. Vast beyond figures. Can't sell it, can't sell it? Don't you see, my dear sir, that your talk is idiocy. You are saying that the human race no longer needs food, no longer wants shelter or clothes or warmth, or light or heat or power. If we can't sell it abroad, let's all go out there and eat it. If foreigners don't want houses, let's go and live in them. If no one wants light, let's sit in a flood of it and laugh.

Of course immigration must be organized: what's true of the mass is not true of the single man. Put one immigrant down in Victoria by himself with nothing more to it than that and of course its only one more man without a job. You'll have to board him at the Empress Hotel: and he'll never leave.

Nor does it follow that the system of immigration needed now, is the same as was needed fifty years ago. The 'homestead system' ran its course and finished it. The essence of it lay in the idea that if the immigrant were offered free land, of a kind that needed no clearing and was ready for instant cultivation, he would then find his way to it, and would sell his produce in a market practically unlimited. His coming to the country would automatically bring, without state aid, the crowd of shopkeepers, middle men, parasites (lawyers, clergymen, professors, etc.) who completed the environment. This was the famous Homestead System which we adopted from the United States in North West Canada in 1875.

But the situation is no longer there. In the States all the free land of that class is gone, every acre if it: in Canada a great deal. And what is more, the immigrant cannot find the money to come. Put the steamship fares at ten dollars a head and there are twenty million people in Europe who can't pay it. The homestead system is a hopeless misfit in a world of doles and relief and collapsed markets.

But there are other systems, both public,— depending on the state,—and private,—depending on the inducement of profit. What many people do not know is that before the Homestead System, by its temporary appropriateness and its success, drove all others from the field, there were other systems some in full operation, others in an opening stage.

There is the 'religious' system, the motive pertaining to the next world but this. To it belong the Rappites of Indiana, the Shakers of Oneida and the Mormons of the Golden Temple and the Salt Sea. Of all systems it is economically the most successful. But we are not religious enough for it. There is the Wakefield system, initiated with considerable success in Canterbury Province, New Zealand and parodied in South Australia (1836). Gibbon Wakefield's idea (he got it in prison where bright ideas come easy) was that the immigrant should have all his expenses paid, turn into a hired man, save his money, buy land, make money, hire another immigrant, and so on like a school girl's chain letter to unknown gentlemen. What is more, the system *can* work and did work and will work again.

But it could be properly combined with the other system that worked with such extraordinary success in Upper Canada a hundred years ago. This was the system of land companies like the old Canada Company of John Galt and his associates, chartered in 1824. There people received the right to settle a tract of land,—in their case in the western peninsula of Ontario: they received proprietory rights on the soil and timber: they were pledged to bring out settlers: as part of the bargain they built roads, churches and schools: but they got exemption from taxes. Their reward,—apart from moral gratification,—lay in the fact that they scooped off what was afterwards called the 'unearned increment'.

The company founded thus Galt and Stratford and Guelph, put 4,500 settlers into the Huron district and made lots of money. If the academic socialists are right they were all 'bourgeoisie' and no doubt went to hell. But it was worth it.

I like to recall some of the scenes of their incoming and to realize how easily, if we were so minded, it could be all done again.

"As the sun set on a summer evening of 1827 Galt and his associates stood in the forest and with the axe passed from hand to hand, they felled on

*a rising knoll a great maple tree to mark the site
of a town. This done the axe was exchanged for
a circulating flask of whiskey and a health was
drunk to the prosperity of the future city—the
present city—of Guelph."*

But there remains still another plan of immigration which so far as I know never had a
name but which filled a large part in the development of earlier Canada. It might be called the
Manorial system. What happened was this. People of the landed class, not quite rich enough to
live at home, or having no land because of being
younger sons, came out to Canada. They wanted
country life, not the life of the working peasants
but of landed gentry. To many people, of whom
I am humbly one, this is the most fascinating, the
most natural of all human activities: and it gives
full scope to the activities of women as of men:
it is the best life in the world for health, for
children, for peace of mind. The seasons come
and go, the planted hedges and the drooping elms
take on antiquity: the grass grows smooth on the
wide lawn. Outside it all, the world is well forgotten.

Such homes were made in Canada by people of
family and substance,—people let us be bold even
if we go to hell for it,—of the better class. They
brought their servants and their labourers, imported cottagers and settled down on wide estates
of five hundred to a thousand acres (wide for Canada, not England) to reproduce again the homes
and the life they knew. The system failed here.

The estates broke up. Democracy called the cottagers. The public school for all leveled up and
leveled down. The 'gentleman' lost his money,
grew shabby and turned into a tavern bum with
an Oxford accent. As a child I remember lots of
them.

We need the bums back. Coiled up in their
method was a mainspring of vital truth. What
we need is a 'back to the land' system, not merely
for the working people of the labour class but for
people with a little money. What spells poverty
in a modern city crammed with luxury and every
breath a dollar, is peace and comfort in the
country. A man miserable on a city pension, or a
retired, over-rich business man belching in his
club, could be a manorial king on a country estate,
up with lark, as busy and as useless. All we need
is to bring back again the lost art of how to lose
money like a gentleman.

*   *   *   *   *

But I can go no further with the topic here.
I keep it for a more sustained chapter on Migration and Settlement. Immigration is our need
and our opportunity.

CHAPTER ELEVEN

THE ISLAND OF THE BLEST

Vancouver Island—The Last Word in Charm
of Climate—English Summer and Pickwickian
Winter—The Lost Glory and the New Future
of Victoria—Manorial Settlement on Vancouver Island—Losing Money Like a Gentleman.

There is no doubt that Vancouver Island represents the last word in charm and beauty of scenery.

I stood looking out from the deck of the steamer
as we drew near, at the varied scene of island,
mountain and sanded beach that dotted the sunlit
waters of Juan de Fuca Strait.

"So this," I said to Captain Bob McMurray
who was beside me, "This is Vancouver Island!"
Just that,—I could find no other way to express
it—"This is Vancouver Island!"

"No," he said, "not that, that's the United
States."

"Well, at any rate," I said, "*that* is Vancouver
Island,—beautiful!"

"Yes," he said, "it reminds me of the Hebrides."

"Everything does," I said.

*   *   *   *   *

But there is no doubt of the instantaneous impression of peace and rest that the Island gives.
No wonder that so many retired people, pensioned
people make their homes in its chief city of
Victoria.

For example (to run ahead of the steamer a

minute) at a dinner presently given in my honour
by a lot of 'old boys' (very much so) of my old
school, I noted that one half—exactly and literally one half,—of the guests present were retired
Colonels. The other half, poor fellows, were
only Majors. There were two Generals on the
list but they wouldn't come.

It is very different out on the prairies. There
all the elderly men of dignity and consequence are
medical men. The rest are dead.

But what I failed to meet either on the prairies
or the Island were men of my own particular
rank, retired professors. I commented on this at
the dinner of which I speak and they told me that
there was a retired professor, (also of economies)
at the Mental Hospital up at Ulgettit on the
Island, (pronounced *you'll get it*). They said I
ought to go there.

It is odd, by the way, that on the Island they
have a whole lot of names like that, Indian names,
with the 'U' prouounced out in full as 'You';—
such as Ucluit, and Uquittit, and Ucheesit and
others I don't remember. British Columbian
Indian names are very easy: the natives' minds are
simple; they had to have something they could say
and remember. If they had named the other Canadian places they would have called Quebec, Oceit,
and Montreal, Owatalotofit and Toronto, Dont-
mentionit.

But as I was saying, Vancouver Island with the
city of Victoria that lies at the foot of it, represents the last word in charm of climate and in

beauty.   Beyond it, till we reach another world, is nothing.   Here is the long slow spring of England, lingering over its early flowers: here the wet tears of April sunshine weeping for a winter that never was; a luxuriant summer that blossoms but never burns; autumn mellow with mist and fruit; and well in time to make an English Christmas, a mimic winter, with a tang of frost in the air, a make believe snowstorm, with angry threatenings that dissolve again into sunshine.   Such a Christmas and such a winter as a Charles Dickens might love, a truly Pickwickian season.

It has been said of good old George the Third, I think by Thackeray, that when he was in the country, he was always up betimes, and always early in the open air, and feeling happy, and that when he came to a building, or a bridge or such, he used to ask any little boys that were about, 'What bridge is this?'   And when they told him, he would say, 'Then let's give three cheers for it!' George the Third should have lived in Victoria in the winter sunshine.   He'd have cheered his old head off every morning.   I understand that the thermometer gives Victoria a winter day-time temperature of 42 degrees, and that taking the average of all the year round there is sunshine for about six hours a day which is almost twice what they get in a year in London.   But the thermometer and the barometer are the least part of it.   It's the feeling that matters.

And with it all is the sight and sound of the sea; in wide harbours, in crooked inlets and deep gorges, always the sea.   Turn aside but a few steps from the sound of the traffic of Victoria and you can hear the sea pounding on the beaches below. There it is, always, south and east and west, and across the water that is ruffled and flecked with foam rises the impressive outline of the Olympics in the State of Washington with eternal sunshine in their snow-covered tops.   For Vancouver Island, the lower twenty or thirty miles of it with Victoria and the chief settlement, is not on the Pacific Ocean.   It is 'on' the United States.   It sits inside the arm of the State of Washington like a ball in a cup.   Here is no place for the roar and clatter of commerce.   If Victoria ever had a 'commercial future', it lost it long ago in favour to the mainland of Vancouver; as witness the old docks falling to decay, the long warehouses unused, the ghost of by-gone wholesale houses and the lustre-less emblems of what was once 'Chinatown'.

This is no place for *work*.   This is a place where not to work; a place for happy people, for tired people, for frozen people from the prairies, for happy lovers on honeymoon to find the shady valleys and the crooked paths in the woods and the solitary beaches that murmur as softly as the voice of love itself; a place for harrassed people over worn with work and needing to be re-made; and above all the last abiding place on earth for people whose work is done to sit out their hour in the sunset.

*   *   *   *   *

All of such detail of climate and scenery can be

turned from the warm diction of rhetoric to the cold language of facts after this fashion.

Vancouver Island lies in a general direction of northeast to southwest along the coast of British Columbia for some two hundred and eighty miles. It has an area of 12,408 square miles which makes it a quarter of the size of England and rather more than the size of Belgium. Its Canadian counterpart on the east coast, Prince Edward Island, has only 2,184 square miles. It is separated from the mainland by narrow and torturous channels at its northern extremity which widen in the middle space to the broad Gulf of Georgia across which the distance from Nanaimo to Vancouver City on the mainland is a distance of thirty-six miles. The Island projects down below the international boundary line of forty-nine degrees north, as far as latitude 48° 20′ and hence the mainland of the United States surrounds all the lower part of the island. The coast line of the island is deeply broken and indented with inlets and river mouths, especially on the west side, facing the open Pacific, where communication is only possible by sea. On the east side a railway runs north from Victoria through Nanaimo to Courtenay, a total length of 139 miles, with two little side branches. All the upper half of the island and all the west side is without railroads. There are excellent motor roads in all directions, very much in all directions, round greater Victoria, and a motor road up the east coast for 90 miles. On the west coast there is a road to Jordan River, 42 miles, and one or two disconnected bits further on.   But apart from that, access to the west and north is only by the sea.

The climate is singularly mild and equable reproducing that of the Cornish Riviera or the district of the Pyrenees around Biarritz.   Unlike the mainland of British Columbia, the island has no decided 'rainy season' but enjoys much sunshine even in the winter months.   The snow fall is merely occasional and never lingers.

The Island is densely wooded, especially with evergreen, coniferous trees,—great spruce and cedars are seen everywhere: even in the city park of Victoria there are plenty of evergreen trees two and three hundred years old.   The grass keeps bright all winter, there is a wealth of ferns, arbutus and other perennial greens, so that the winter aspect of the Island conveys no sense of desolation.   In summer, hills and valleys alike are embowered in the beautiful foliage of elms and oaks.   The waters about the Island are tempered by the current from across the Pacific.   They are never very warm nor very cold.   Even in summer the water,—except in shallow beaches,—is cool and invigorating rather than luxurious and warm.   Ice comes and goes on the pools and ponds and snow irregularly covers the higher hills.

The broken and sheltered waters are admirable for yachting and for motor boating, and in the lonelier reaches afford wonderful fishing,—for salmon in the inlets, for trout in the lakes.   The soil, especially in the sheltered and sunken valleys, is singularly rich; fruit grows in great luxuriance, and the market gardener has no other problem than that of superabundance.

At present the city of Victoria contains some 45,000 souls, or including Esquimalt and the district around to make up Greater Victoria, over 60,000, and the whole Island of Vancouver 130,000. Much of the northern interior is rough, unbroken country, heavily timbered and practically uninhabited. The island has, as said, an area of 12,408 square miles, equal to nearly half of Scotland (30,000). It is interesting to reflect that in point of 'roughness' Vancouver Island has nothing on Scotland. We have for that the word of Scotland's own bard, whose assertion that Caledonia is 'stern and wild' has never been contradicted. Scotland lies further north, the bottom of it about 250 miles above the top of Vancouver; in total resources, even including the coastal fisheries, there is no comparison. Yet Scotland carries a population of 5,000,000 people and helps to make the history and sing the songs of the world. Nearly all of Vancouver Island,—nearly all,—still lies silent, the soft airs of its Pacific climate blowing over it and the ocean murmuring below its primeval pines. Outside of the populated southern and eastern district, to include Greater Victoria, Nanaimo and Cumberland,—it has only 14,000 inhabitants thinly spread on the edges and outline of 10,000 square miles !

How long will Canadians remain asleep, in this silly dream that our country is full?

*   *   *   *   *

There,—That is the background, either hot or cold. That's the Island of Vancouver and its capital city, Victoria. What is to be the future, and how is the Island to fit into our Canadian economic life?

At present there are two islands, Prince Edward and Vancouver, at the opposite ends of our confederation, each blessed by nature in soil and climate, each a fit abode for human happiness. Jacques Cartier said of Prince Edward Island, "It needs only the nightingale!" I don't think Vancouver Island needs even that; the local crow is good enough.

But each of these islands has been brought from its high hopes to a state of stagnation, an arrested development, where the high cost of living forbids alike the leisure of retirement or the mock-activity of gentleman-farming. Each blames the situation on its connection with the other provinces.

What are we to do about it? Now the islands cannot expect to 'have it coming and going.' It is no use talking in one breath of Vancouver and Charlottetown as great seats for manufacture, as each a future metropolis of industry, and in the next breath to talk of Vancouver Island or Prince Edward Island as wonderful places to retire to, a haven for people of modest means, a home for landed gentry dispossessed in England by lack of land and the rise of taxes. It is, I think, that fundamental contradiction of trying to think two things at once that is responsible for much of the perplexity of Victoria,—for I speak at present only of the western situation.

Vancouver Island,—I will put it very plainly,— is suffering, as said, from an arrested development. The old ambitions are frustrated, the new ones not yet entertained. Vancouver Island was once a 'colony' by itself. Victoria was, and is, a capital. Victoria saw itself as a great Pacific seaport, a rival of Sydney, Melbourne and Hong-Kong. Vancouver City on the mainland eclipsed that ambition and took over that role. The sooner Victoria understands that the eclipse is final, the better for it.

A metropolis of the sea cannot any longer be on an island without bridge and rail connections with the mainland. In the past it was otherwise. Other things counted more. In the days of sailing ships, pirates and unfriendly savages, safety came first, and islands such as Manhattan and Montreal were ideal for easy approach and efficacious defense. With the altered epoch they threw bridges and drove tunnels to the mainland and became part of it. Trains and ships exchange their freights and cargoes. Hong-Kong still keeps its insular isolation. But when railroads and industrial civilization really reach China it is all over with Hong-Kong.

So with Victoria.

The only industries that can flourish on the island are those crude 'extractive' industries of lumber, coal and mineral and fish that have nothing to do with tariff protection and urban con-

centration. It is claimed that there are 127 billion
feet of merchantable timber on Vancouver Island
within reach of deep water harbours: that the coal
deposits of Nanaimo, Comox and the vicinity are
estimated at 1,178 million tons within an area of
185 square miles, with probably six times as much
on the island: the fisheries of the west coast
are inexhaustible assets. All that is admirable:
and all the better if the island attracts a new flow
if immigrants who need cheap houses and cheap
fuel and cheap food.

Yet even with all these wonders of climate and
native resources it is doubtful if there would be
any great development for Vancouver Island if it
were left on the same footing, as the rest of Canada. I mean, under a regime of high protection
to manufactures, high costs of living, heavy
burden of debt. For all of these things, if they
are not over-done, we have in Central Canada
counterbalancing advantages; the protective tariff
means a greater manufacturing population and it
means that people live here instead of living somewhere else. But the argument has no application
to Vancouver Island any more than it has to
Prince Edward Island. Our high tariff hits it a
blow for which it has hardly any 'come-back'.
With us in Central Canada high cost can be offset,—we hope,—by high wages and salaries. On
the Island it prevents the incoming of the very
people most needed and most suited, people from
the old country with a little money of their own.

*   *   *   *   *

Therefore I do not think that Vancouver Island can stay in Canada under present conditions without losing a lot of its natural advantages. It does not fit in with our tariff policy, manufacturing policy and our economic nationalism.

It has been suggested that Victoria might be a 'free port'. Lately the phrase 'free port' is widely heard, though little understood, in Canada. In the complete sense it means a duty-free area,—let us imagine it the Island of Montreal,—which includes factories, workers and residents, makes all costs cheap, even cost of labour, (in terms of money) and so promotes export. But this sense implies a tariff boundary against the rest of Canada; or else a huge advantage over all other Canadian sites: and also means that the people on the 'free port', say the one million people of Montreal Island, buy cheap foreign goods and the Canadian manufacturer loses their custom. The other kind of free port,—such as the existing area in New York,—merely means the extension of the bounded warehouse idea to a factory. It promotes the import of cheap goods and their manufacture in the area for foreign export. But all this goes little further than a system of drawbacks of duty on goods imported for manufacture and export. We have that now.

None of this fits Victoria. A free port with free entry of goods to Canada would merely substitute, for the rest of us, high cost of transport in place of high cost of manufacture.

What is needed for the whole Island is a relief of the cost of living so as to make it a goal for emigration of people of moderate means anxious to live on their own.   It is no use to try to make it a playground of the rich.   Apart from a few hotels that does not go far.   There are not enough millionaires.   Money, big money, is not made from the rich: it is made from the poor.   Pennies and cents make plutocrats.

Here is what I would do if I could have the statute book of British Columbia to write in for ten minutes, with an iron pen that could write what no one must rule out.

First I would give a lot of tariff relief to cut the cost of living.   I think specially of motor cars for non-commercial use.   An island is an island. Motor cars can't fly.   That makes administration automatic, and fraud, with proper registration, very difficult.

Then I would cut the cost of clothes.   It seems a wicked thing to say in Canada but I'd even take the tariff off a man's shirt.   I would add wide and sweeping exemption of settlers' effects in the biggest sense.

Then I would grant a ten years' exemption of income tax to all immigrants from the old country who brought over, such and such family and such and such servants, cottagers and dependents. This would involve moving their capital from England, or else the English tax would take it.   I would make the condition that if they moved it, it must be moved to the Island.

I would have a list of approved securities, municipal and corporate, recommended under provincial accountants, and even, perhaps, of guaranteed 4 per cent. securities, (shooting all Social Crediters during the partridge season).

On these terms I would offer land in lots of ten, fifty, or five hundred acres. The idea would not be for commercial farming but for resident settlement, for what used to be called 'gentleman-farming',—that glorious method of losing money slowly instead of fast, which distinguishes the English gentleman from the American business man.

Why give these people ten years' exemption from the income tax, protests the Canadian patriot, when the rest of us pay it? Because that will make them come: without that they won't. They bring their capital, they bring what is called in Alberta their 'purchasing power'. Best and most priceless of all they bring their *children* to grow up as British Canadians. That is the greatest asset of all. I know this for I came to Canada as such a child sixty-one years ago: when I think what an asset I have been I realize that I sold out too cheaply. I should have charged money for coming. And anyway what is ten years? We give a similar exemtpion for a factory to settle in a town,—why not to the makers of a nation?

* * * * *

This would set in motion a wave of what I have called elsewhere manorial settlement, the establishment of people of means, loving the country life, fond of what they call work and never having really worked a day in their existance.   Work is when you go in somewhere at seven or eight o'clock in the morning and the boss says 'do this', and you do it until noon.   He says 'I want so and so' and you mustn't say 'Do you'? I have worked once or twice.   It's awful.   The Indians were quite right about it: it's beneath a human being.

But work that means poking and pottering round a little place of ten to twenty acres, with gardens, orchards, firewood and home brewed beer! that is something else!   And the cottagers and dependents?   They don't work either: each runs his own little show.

Such is the small estate.   Imagine how eagerly people in England with an income of say five hundred pounds a year,—after paying about a quarter as much for taxes, and getting by investment only three per cent.,—how eagerly they would turn to such an Island of the Blest.   And the thing is there.   It's easy.

Manorial settlement is not buying and selling,—a minimum of that.   It is as nearly self-sufficing as can be.   People who talk of 'mixed farming' are trying to express the idea.   Under such settlement you own your house and land and so there is no rent: fuel costs nothing: food next to nothing: if the tax is off your shirt it's cheap enough.   Electric light isn't needed.   Napoleon never had it.   Telephones can be fixed up locally. Local roads can be made and kept up by joint labour, as we used to do in Ontario and still do a little. Bridges can be maintained by tolls and schools by fees and subscriptions. In other words, there is hardly any need for local taxes.

The number of people attracted would be enormous *provided* they have faith in the credit and good faith of the Island. I would help this by offering facilities to 'come and see': a refund say of one-half the rail and steamer fare if the people took a trial trip and then come to settle. The amount of incoming money would boom the lumber and building trades, and the trade in golf clubs, playing cards, Scotch whiskey, shot guns, waders, fishing rods and all the apparatus of English land settlement.

With such a plan the central idea is everything,—the manorial settlement of Vancouver Island,—the 'details' are nothing. In thirty-five years of college and public lecturing I always refused to discuss details. It's too late to start now. Let the idea stand for itself.

CHAPTER TWELVE

PROVINCES AND DOMINION

Our Increasing Economic Separatism—Is Canada Breaking Up?—The Original Union of 1867—Central Power to Escape American Sin—Things Go the Other Way—The United States Unified—Canada Balkanized—All Seceding at Once—Ways and Means of Salvation.

I want to state a case,—as my friends among the clergy like to put it,—'fearless of denial'. That means, to overstate it in such strong language that no one dares contradict it. I want to show that Canada is in danger of breaking up: that the provinces have utterly outgrown, or overpassed, the place intended for them: that they are planets threatening to leave their orbits. In other words, it is to me visible and obvious that Canada has already changed from a federation to a confederacy. It is now threatening to turn into a sort of confederate league, a union of commonwealths, a 'heptarchy'.

Worse than that; during the transition so much doubt envelops the question of rival powers,—legal doubt as to where the provinces end and the Dominion begins,—that we stand arrested, brought to a full stop, thrown into Chancery. The Dominion undertook to legislate a general code (1935) on labour and wages and social security. What happened? The statutes drifted through the courts. Most of them as enacted were declared *ultra vires* by the Privy Council and no one knows now what authority can make general regulation of labour in Canada and whether any one can. The legislation proposed may have been good or may have been bad. Similarly Alberta by an executive order and an Act (1936), and others described above, followed by other legislation (Reduction and Settlement), under-took to cancel half the interest of public debt, to lower municipal debt interest, and to cancel in part all private debts more than three years old. The legislation may have been good, may have been bad. That's not the point. The Alberta courts (February 1937), declared the legislation beyond the consti-tution power of Alberta: perhaps it was, perhaps it wasn't. The province is proposing to answer by legislation doing the same thing in another way, cancelling interest instead of principal. The decisions are not final and the situation must drag on till at last, say in a year or two, the Privy Council gives a decision. By the time it does, something else will have happened.

To all this there is no end. We are in Chancery as solidly and hopeless as were Jarndyce and Jarndyce; worse, because they knew it, some of them, and we don't. It is strange how history re-peats itself and the people repeating it don't know it. We look back with a smile to the old Court of Chancery with its infinite delays, and don't know that we are in it ourselves. We are in as tight as ever was a Jarndyce. We are like a lion in a net, a Laocoon coiled with snakes. To the lawyers the coil is an embrace. They like it. The Lord Chief Justice of England wrote a book in 1934 called the *New Despotism*, to show how beautiful is the system of appeal to the courts and how wicked an executive decision by an official. The Lord Justice missed the point. Appeal means infinite delay, uncertain paralysis like that which lies heavy on Canada right now. An executive decision is as final as a headsman's axe. He should read his British history again and he would see where that headsman's axe comes in with its beautiful finality. At least the case is over. It is what the lawyers call a *res judicata*. 'Stone dead,' said Lord Strafford of the Stuart tyranny, 'hath no fellow'. Later he 'got his'.

But as it is we sit in Chancery with all the numbness that goes with it. The Dominion cabinet could have nullified the whole Alberta legislation, not *qua ultra vires,* but as "not in the general interests of the Dominion", a power expressly granted with a full understanding of what it meant, and expressly set forth and annotated by Sir John A. Macdonald as Attorney-General in 1869. But no Dominion Government,—Liberal, Conservative or Apostolic,—dares use the power now.

More still than that. We don't know how to amend or change our constitution. We chained it around us and lost the key of the padlock. In 1867 the recourse to the plenary power of the British Parliament seemed enough: so it was for a little while: joint addresses and an Imperial Act (as in 1870, 1871, 1884, etc.) was all that was needed. Easy and simple and so much better than noisy American voting, or a French coup d'état.

The British North America Act, which is the backbone of our constitution, was framed in 1865 in Canada and enacted in England in 1867. The form it took reflected our relation to the United States. That the union was made at all, was due to the fear of American aggression. It took its peculiar form,—supposed to be centralization,— as an effort to keep away from American sin,— state rights. So much that we have done in Canada has been based on this idea of keeping clean of American sin, and yet we always get nearer to it. The Loyalists of 1784 came here to try not to be Americans. Governor Simcoe opened his little Niagara parliament of 1792 as an "image and transcription" of British government. Lord Durham diagnosed our sickly condition in 1839 as needing a dose of the British system of responsible government. Confederation, as made, was an attempt to get as close to the unitary system of British government, all powerful at the centre in the last resort, as the physical, racial and religious circumstances allowed. The unification of economic life was a thing everybody took for granted. The safeguarding of language, of schools, of religion was the reason for the federatism of the compact. Economics didn't come in.

Everything went the other way. The Americans killed states rights' with the sword. When it came to life again as 'economic rights' they killed it with constitutional amendments and decisions of the courts (Income Tax Amendments of 1913, etc., etc.). Now, to extripate the last of the economic heresy, Mr. Roosevelt, like a Plantagenet king sends the judges of the Supreme Court to the block. As with ourselves and the court of Chancery, Mr. Roosevelt repeats history. 'Fore God!' said the King, the actual words are those of Richard III, as Protector, "I will not dine until your head is off." Little children reading history often wonder how the King could behead the meek old men. Wiser people knew then, and know now, that very often meek old men need beheading the worst way. The man who orders it was called a 'tyrant' in Greece, a 'dictator' in Rome, a 'despotic monarch' in Tudor times, and today a 'business executive'.

So in the United States, the original American sin of divided economic power and state control of economic life, is being ironed out flat into a national unity,—which will bring an advance that will leave us nowhere, if we do not imitate it.

But, contrary to what happened in the United States, since its organization under the British North America Act of 1867, the Dominion of Canada has developed in exactly the contrary direction from that which was intended and expected. The conferences that sat in Charlottetown in 1864 and in Quebec in 1865 to frame the Canadian constitution met under the shadow of the American Civil War. Before their eyes was an evidence of the disasters that accompany divided power and the lack of sovereign authority. They intended to avoid such disasters for Canada by giving the central government an overwhelming power and in especially conferring on it the whole range of economic control (B.N.A. Act, 91). They safeguarded the rights of provinces and of minorities in regard to religion and language, but gave, as they thought, the final control of natural economic life to the Dominion. The taxation clause, as contrasted with the limited powers of the United States Congress, gave to the federal government the right of taxation by "any mode or system"; it received the plenary control of trade and commerce, including the customs and the excise; of the criminal law; of money and banking; of immigration (concurrent but over-riding); of land-settlement in the North-West in which the Hudson's Bay Company was to transfer its vast empty holdings that later made three provinces.

Nothing was said about labour legislation, labour disputes, etc., because in 1867 no one was thinking of such. The clause which gave to the provinces (92) the control of "property and civil rights" meant presumably nothing more than the regulation of purchase, sale, and the taxation of inheritance and real estate. Later on this clause was destined to swallow up all the others. It is hardly conceivable that in 1867 anybody could imagine that the clause could enable a province to tear up a contract made by itself in good faith

with a corporation of another province. The only
fear at first was that the province would be too
feeble financially to exist. Hence the system
whereby they received 'subsidies' as their chief
means of support. In the year 1868 the whole
expenditure of Ontario was $1,179,269, and the
whole expenditure of Quebec was $1,181,932.
Nearly the whole of this expenditure was defrayed
by Dominion subsidies.

The B.N.A. Act went into effect: the North-
West was taken over (1869) : a tiny province (the
'postage stamp' of Manitoba of 1870) was carved
out of it. British Columbia came in (1871),
on the promise of getting a railroad, Prince
Edward Island (1873) on the promise of getting
rid of one. The power of the Dominion grew at
first like a vigorous tree. It bound up the whole
country in a 'National Policy' of high protection;
it put a railway to the Pacific, 1886: it poured
emigrants into the North-West, especially after
1896, in a veritable flood, an "invasion" alike
from Europe and from America. The best politicians, the really national figures, the Lauriers,
the Blakes, the Siftons, left the provinces for Ottawa. The provincial legislatures seemed turning
into 'sun-dogs' of the over-bright illumination
from the capital.

But unforseen and unnoticed great changes
came. The discovery of mineral wealth, under-
provincial control, literally changed the map of
Canada, and turned wilderness to Eldorado. In
Confederation days Canada produced only about

$1,000,000 worth of gold per annum: (some 50,000 fine ounces), in 1935 it had passed beyond 3,000,000 fine ounces and was second only to South Africa in world production; in silver it is second only to Mexico. The water-power of Canada, an asset rising in importance as petroleum plays out, represents 34,000,000 horse-power, all of it—except 731,000 in the Arctic—under the control of the provinces. The enormous pulp and paper industry, unknown at Confederation, has become a vast provincial concern. At times a Canadian province dictates news-print prices to a submissive continent. Add to this the motor-car industry, which while gasoline lasts, affords, along with the monopoly of the sale of liquor, a colossal financial resource.

The result is that the Canadian provinces have turned into little economic kingdoms. Ontario has an area of 415,582 square miles and a population of 3,500,000. It has opened up a railway of its own, tapping minerals and forest resources, northward to the shallow and lonely shores of the James Bay. It has more than 600 miles of sea-coast. An air-fleet floats over it, looking down to find gold. The province owns all the public lands, the Dominion none: owns the forests and the minerals. It has an annual expenditure of over $60,000,000. It does not control money and legal tender, but, like its sister province, Quebec, it contains trust and loan companies as powerful instruments of credit. The province, not the Dominion, has the control of all municipal institutions: the city of Montreal, with a million people, must take the medicine given to it from Quebec. Enthroned over this sovereignty is the prime minister of the province, like the 'Great King' of of the Persians,. These men—the Tachereaus and the Duplessis and the Fergusons and the Hepburns—go no longer to Ottawa, except as ambassadors from their kingdoms.

More than that, we seem to have been doing our best to augment in every way the power of the provinces, to depress in every way the power of the Dominion. To the Dominion was given at Confederation the power to set aside provincial legislation if it was contrary to the general interests of the Dominion. This has nothing to do with the right of the courts to set aside provincial legislation that goes beyond the powers allotted to the provinces. It is supplementary to it, intended to begin where the other ended, as equity used to supplement the common law.

This power was vigorously used. In the years 1900-1905 the Dominion disallowed a series of British Columbia statutes intended to restrict oriental immigration. Probably the Dominion was wrong in its policy. But it was right in its law. The Dominion *could have* set aside two years ago the Ontario Acts cancelling power contracts: *could have,* but as things go now, wouldn't dare to. The Dominion could set aside the whole Alberta debt cancellation: *could,* in point of law, but in point of fact is not likely to. The passage of an actual Social Credit Act (a help-

yourself dividend) might rouse its enfeebled
energy to action.

The courts have joined in. The mystic clause
for "control of property and civil rights" (B.N.A.
Act 92 par. 13), as mystic as a Delphic Oracle
has been worked by the attendant priests with as
great a latitude. Under this clause provinces are
now able, among other things, to tax one another's
goods. Manitoba levies an import duty on Ontario beer: that is the plain meaning of the supplementary five cents a bottle extra paid in drink-
ing it.

The climax was reached when the Privy Council declared *ultra vires* the code of Dominion legislation adopted in 1935 to regulate labour and
wages, the Minimum Wage Act, the Weekly Rest
in Industrial Undertakings Act, the Limitation
of Hours of Work Act, the Employment and
Social Insurance Act. To most of us here in Canada who have devoted long and arduous years to
the study of our history and to the meaning and
purpose of the British North American Act, the
decision seems absolutely erroneous,—bad law,
bad sense, entire ignorance of what was meant
and intended in 1867. Is it not time that these
appeals to the Privy Council, in such a case as
this appeals from wisdom to ignorance, from interest to indifference, should end? Why is such
an appeal necessary? Have we not courts and
lawyers and honesty? Granted that the Privy
Council is wonderful in deciding the law of
Nigeria as between the Native Sheik El Fooselum

and Tribal Chief Yum-Bumbo, are we quite in
their class? I know at least two Canadian Chief
Justices, one retired and one active, who could
give a better decision on Canadian constitutional
questions than the whole Privy Council. Make
it three. I've thought of one out West.

Where custom failed and the courts failed to increase provincial power we have done it by Dominion legislation, a sort of Hari-Kari. The
public land of the North-West belonged to the
Dominion. With that understanding the people
of the Dominion at large paid for putting railways across the continent. In 1931 the public
land of Alberta and Saskatchewan was 'given
back' to them with a compensation of $6,250,000
for our having dared to use it. Henceforth the
Dominion is powerless to organize and estimate
immigration, except into the arctic regions. It
has no land.

What has Ottawa got left, in the way of
economic control? Very little. It never had the
public lands and resources of the older provinces,
it has given over to provincial control those of
the new. It controls immigration, but without
land for immigrants. This means that it has the
right to shut out immigrants, but no satisfactory
way to let them in. It controls the navy—but
there isn't any to speak of—and the army—what
there is of it: controls defence on a continent still
happy in peace. It hunts and hangs criminals.
It keeps track of the weather; adds up statistics
(marvellously well; its Year Book is a model);

it runs experimental farms. But the economic life of the country has passed beyond its control.

This economic disunion works like an evil leaven in the body corporate of the state. Like a malignant disease, the worse it is the worse it tends to be. The demand is for further separatism, for the breaking of the union, or the imposition of new terms as the price of consenting to stay in. The sorrows of the Maritimes are too well known to need rehearsal. But now comes the demand for secession in the very heart of French Canada,— the parent home of our commonwealth. It is as if the nest wanted to leave the young birds, the odd homestead to get up and walk away. It seems incredible but a lot of younger French-Canadians talk now of 'Laurentia',—a republic on the St. Lawrence. It is a dream that vanishes on waking, a bubble that bursts at a touch. How could French Canada secede without Montreal? And how could it secede *with* Montreal? Does Laurentia take with it the English banks and the magnates and McGill University with its professors, both active and super-active? Will the Republic hold and control the St. Lawrence, dictating to 125,000,000 other people? Or will Laurentia put on the old-time mantle of poverty and devotion and retire to the snows of the Peribonka, in the land of Maria Chapdelaine?

Nor does the list of secessions end there. At times New Ontario finds Old Ontario too old and proposes to quit it. Look at this from the wrong angle and it looks right,—Fort William as the capital, the mining country as the kingdom and no limit but the sky! But like all the other secessions, it takes for granted the passive co-operation of the rest of Canada,—the continuance of rail, trade and tariff freedom,—nothing changed except its own secession.

Of similar aspect is the 'secession' of Victoria already discussed. Of the Queen Charlotte Islands I have not heard. They may be going or they may be staying.

CHAPTER THIRTEEN

OUR RAILWAY MUDDLE

A Discussion Without Profanity—The Golden Age of the Intercolonial—From Nowhere to Nowhere or the National Transcontinental—Debt and Deficit—John Willett Chalks up the Score.

The Canadian railway problem represents such a muddle, that it isn't even worth while getting angry about it. I remember being rebuked some years ago for so doing. I had written in a very bitter strain about the year's operation of the Canadian National System and had said sarcastically, "We don't need this railway and by all accounts the Chinese are badly in need of railways. Let's give them the Canadian National." A correspondent of the newspaper, a retired clergyman, wrote and said, "Professor Leacock's suggestion seems excellent: but has he considered the physical difficulty involved on the transfer?"

That's the spirit, that gentle attitude in which to approach a topic so controversial and around which there has been so much bitterness.

I must plead guilty to taking a one-sided view. I have always been against the present Canadian system of make-believe competition as between a railway 'company' that isn't a company at all, but a government department, and a railway company that doesn't get a chance to be one.

But I will write with as little bitterness as possible. I am reminded here of my good old friend

Archie McKinnon whom I knew in Beaverton nearly fifty years ago. Archie was the real type of local politician, a liberal, a 'grit', unchangeable, unconvincible. He was of a great age, had been a rebel in 1837 and had reached a time of life when even a Scotchman begins to feel the ravages of time. But the fire burned in him still.

I met him one day, when the question of a new 'town hall' had reached a fever point of controversy. Archie was standing, leaning on his stick, on the sidewalk, in deep, hard thought. It was a rainy day. But he hadn't noticed it.

I asked him,—

"Mr. McKinnon, what do you think of this town-hall question?"

He turned and answered, —

"Mr. Leacock, my time is short. I am not what I was. And when I go I want to go with no animosity, no bitterness,—with gentleness to all. As to this town-hall question, I prefer to say nothing, absolutely nothing,—ex-c e p t—that there are more damn fools among the Conservatives in Beaverton than would fill an asylum."

                *   *   *   *   *

That's how I feel about our national railways system,—no animosity at all.

So I begin at the beginning. As most people know, there are practically only two railway systems in Canada, the Canadian Pacific Railway Company and the Canadian National Railways. The former is a private corporation, originally incorporated in 1881, generously subsidized with prairie land, and originally, to some extent, with money.   By means of it the North West was opened up, the Atlantic joined to the Pacific, and Confederation rendered geographically possible.

The company, after a hard initial struggle, grew and flourished.   From the time of its inception the company paid dividends in varying amounts until 1911, when the maximum rate of 10 per cent., which was to be maintained until 1932 without a break, was reached.   Its subsidiary enterprises— mines, steamers, hotels—were an added source of revenue.   Its shares—nominally $100 par value—sold as low as $33 in 1895, and sold before the War almost up to $300.   It had the Western field all to itself; the East it shared with feeble competitors.

One of these was the Intercolonial Railway— from Montreal to Halifax—built as a military necessity with the aid of Imperial finance.   Initially it was not expected to make money, and it lived up to the expectation.   The poor mostly rode free, and the rich travelled on passes.   The conductor sat and smoked with the passengers like a ship's captain at his exalted table.

Freight rolled along—when there was any— on its own terms.   The thing was too good not to pass it around.   So when Prince Edward Island was to be coaxed into the Dominion (1873) its bankrupt railway and its ferry service became a part of the Intercolonial.   A rich and rising country carried the burden easily enough, just as a strong man can carry a sore finger.   But the

gangerene was there just the same. It is now working through the whole system.

The other original competitor of the C.P.R. in
Eastern Canada was the Grand Trunk Railway,
intended to link the Great Lakes to the Atlantic, a
company of great opportunities, which it never
realized. It had absorbed a group of minor roads
in Ontario and Quebec. but it never paid a dividend on its Common stock, being managed or
mis-managed, from London. The C.P.R., organized and conducted by a group of men of ex-
ceptional talent and enterprise, was soon able to
compete successfully with the Grand Trunk on
its own ground.

It was this situation which Sir Wilfrid Laurier,
whose true function was benevolence and not business, proposed to turn to political account by
organizing a second transcontinentnal system,
based on the co-operation of the Government and
the Grand Trunk. The Government and the
Grand Trunk were to build a railway from tide
water in New Brunswick (Moncton) to a northern (ready-made) port on the Pacific, presently
called Prince Rupert.

From Moncton to Winnipeg the Government
was to build and own the line, as a National
Transcontinental spanning the St. Lawrence by a
bridge just above Quebec. This was the last
word in American railway construction. In England and in Europe railways were built to connect
existing cities; in America, to connect cities with
others not yet existing—the railway at the start

going from somewhere to nowhere. The railway came first and the towns came after.

This new departure went further. It went from nowhere to nowhere, passing nowhere. It was constructed far north of existing settlement. Its construction reaped a rich harvest for contractors; scandals grew like wild oats along its right-of-way. The western part of the line, from Winnipeg to Prince Rupert, was built by a new company, the Grand Trunk Pacific, its bonds guaranteed to 75 per cent. of its cost. The new company was to rent the National section for fifty years at 3 per cent. of the cost, an agreement by which everybody, except the taxpayer, wanted the cost as high as possible. But the taxpayer, as yet, didn't count. The bridge at Quebec was in the class of the Colossus of Rhodes, equally scenic and about as valuable. The system, operated in conjunction with the Grand Trunk, was a failure from the start, a mill-stone round the neck of Canada.

To make the weight heavier another stone was added. This was the third Transcontinental, the Canadian Northern, built as a private enterprise out of old charters and odd bits, picking up Government and municipal bonuses as a bird picks up crumbs. The Canadian public had lost its head with the boom. The War smashed the whole railway system. But it would have broken anyway of its own weight. By 1916 there were 40,000 miles of railroad in Canada. Here again the frame was too big for the picture.

To save financial disaster the Government took over the Canadian Northern (9,500 miles) in 1917. The Grand Trunk Pacific failed to make its payments. The Dominion took it over. The Grand Trunk collapsed and was taken over in 1920, its shareholders to be paid what their stock was worth. This, in the case of the Common shareholders, turned out to be nothing. Their sobs are not yet hushed. Their fate now stands as a *hodie mihi, cras tibi* for a new set of Common shareholders.

*   *   *   *   *

Out of these elements of historical survival, junk, optimism and extravagance was pretentiously created by Act of Parliament (1923) the Canadian National Railway Company, not a company at all, having neither shares, nor shareholders nor dividends. Its status is that of a little boy given an account book to let him 'pretend'.

The name National Railway Company, adopted in 1919, was later altered to Canadian National Railways. The same childish make-believe of a separate existence was carried on. The government solemnly lent itself money, chalked up debts against itself, and told itself sternly that it really must pay. One recalls the figure, in Dicken's *Barnaby Rudge,* of old John Willett who kept the Maypole Inn and, in his old age, got a knock on the head that made him silly. So he used to stand at his 'tap' serving drinks to his old cronies, and then retired with a wink behind a door and chalk up the score (never paid) on a slate. The Canadian Transportation Department is the old John Willett of Ottawa.

Since that date the Canadian National System has dragged the country further and further into the slough of despond. Supposedly the system pays its operating expenses out of revenue and pays also the interest due on its inherited obligations and on the new money borrowed to maintain and expand it. Whether the operating revenue pays the operating cost is a matter that can be known only to an expert having access to the books. Railway expenditure is hard to check and easy to disguise. Maintenance cost can masquerade as capital cost. Thus the system could show a profit on its operation in reality offset by charges carried to capital. During the last ten years the railway receipts have been reported to cover the cost of operation, save in three depression years, at its highest the net income available for interest was $44,000,000 (1928), and the greatest deficit (1931) was $5,000,000. But the essence of the situation lies elsewhere. The net income available for interest does not suffice to meet the annual interest charge on the securities held by the public and assumed or guaranteed by the Dominion when it took over the railways, let alone the interest on money borrowed directly from the Government. In addition to this, continued expenditure, called 'capital' expenditure, is made by borrowing more money on which again an interest charge must be created. Hence the cumulative deficit, added up as $264,000,000 when the 'Company',—save the mark!—was consolidated in 1923, added up in 1935 to $1,078,000,000.

*   *   *   *   *

This is not the *debt*. This is just the added new deficit by which the original debt is increased. When the constituent lines of the National System were taken over by the Government they owed to the Dominion in return for appropriations, loans, and advances and interest $527,000,000. This by end of 1935 had increased to $1,655,-000,000. In addition to that the National Railways owed to the public at the time of their acquisition the sum of $810,000,000. This had increased by the end of last year to $1,155,-000,000 This is not counting the $247,000,000 rolled up since the Government decided that 'cash' deficits and Eastern lines deficits should not be met by fresh railway borrowings, but by appropriations granted under Act of Parliament.

Meantime in February of the present year the Minister of Transportation presented his report on the operation of the system in 1936. From this it appears that the gross operating revenue was $154,000,000 and the operating income was $145,000,000. This leaves a net revenue after certain other charges of $6,600,000 available towards paying 'fixed charges'. But as the year's fixed charges in the form of interest alone on bonded debt amounted to $49,900,000, this leaves a net income cash deficit of $43,300,000. In addition to this, the government is to lend another $9,916,000 to the railway to spend on 'capital

improvement', and miscellaneous debt require-
ments, and as no one knows where capital improvement ends and current maintenance begins,
without looking at every item, no one can know
how great the real deficit is.   One can only watch
the huge total of debt going steadily up.

But the government doesn't even want people
to watch this: the sight is too painful.   They had
better forget it.   So an Act has been just adopted,
the Reduction of Capital Structure Act of 1937,
to enable us to forget it.   The Act is another
gigantic piece of make-believe.   It is called "re-
organizing the capital structure of the railway".
All it means is blotting out its debts.   It is held
that if the Railway borrows from the government,
and the government borrows from the people to
get the money, then the debt adds up twice, and
makes one dollar of debt look like two.   To avoid
this, the minister rolls up the debt in his hand as
a conjurer does a billiard ball, then opens his hand
and, presto! the debt has vanished.

Consequently from now on, each current addition to the debt is of no consequence.   Provided
always that we can't pay it, we agree to wipe it
off and forget it.

It's a great idea.   I've been thinking of "reorgan-
izing the capital structure of my account with the
University Club on the same plan.

A 'company' run on this plan becomes a
dangerous prodigal.   It has everything to gain
and nothing to lose.   It has no dividends to pay,
nothing to fear, and a fond parent to pay its debts.

It can spend what it likes on equipment, on
luxury, on 'service', and its *alma mater,* the Dominion of Canada, will pay for it. It can build
competing lines, run them at a loss, carry goods
below cost—it doesn't matter. Its finance is that
of a spoiled spendthrift—just ducks and drakes.

*   *   *   *   *

But why, it is asked, does the country stand for
it? Why permit the National System—it has
dropped the word 'company' as too small, too
mean for it—to be a national spoiled darling?
The reason lies in its history. It came into the
world—its original skelton of 1903—just about
the time of the clamour for 'People's' railways, of
opposition to trusts and monopolies. Someone
had called a railway an octopus. The western
farmers didn't want octopi around. They had
pests enough. And perhaps, too, at the height
of its prestige, the existing railway had treated the
West a little bit *de haut en bas,* wouldn't build
branch lines everywhere the farmers wanted them.
At any rate, western agrarian opinion clamoured
for a 'People's' railroad, and still want it. For
the deficit they don't care. Let the 'East' pay it.
They've trouble enough without worrying over
the railway problem. So the whole transportation structure of Canada drifts like a mass of
wreckage, nearer and nearer to the fall. The
Canadian National policy is driving the C.P.R.
towards the edge. Its dividends have stopped; its
shares have fallen. The farmers don't care—

don't realize the danger that, if the crash comes, it comes to them also.

As a consequence there is very little interest in the West of Canada in the railway problem.   A lecture on the subject would be delivered to empty seats.   The Western farmer has somehow got it into his head that the railway problem is a 'good one' on the East.   He is like the Irishman of the anecdote who was carried up ten stories in a hod, for a bet, by a fellow-bricklayer and who said as he paid the money, "At the eighth story I thought I had you."

So the Western farmer, carried up in the hod of the annual budget, peeps over the edge and chuckles "This time he'll drop me sure!"

CHAPTER FOURTEEN

IMMIGRATION AND LAND SETTLEMENT

Immigration spells Prosperity—Must be Organized—Company Settlement—Philanthropy and Rapacity, Half and Half—The Valley of Hope—The Company and the Colonists—A Beautiful Dream, that may Come True.

At various points in this book I have spoken of immigration. I have tried to show, in the first place, that Canada is practically an empty country, as compared with its great latent resources. In a book which I wrote some years ago on *Economic Prosperity in the British Empire* (and which no one ever read except a few prime ministers and some of the older bishops), I placed a map to show our potential population of 250,000,000. It was based on the number of people now living on a similar extent of territory, of no better resources, in Europe. I still think the argument sound. But divide if one will by ten and there will still be room for millions of emigrants.

I have tried elsewhere to show that an imigrant is an asset. Directly or indirectly, he brings to the country a great quantity of 'capital'. Think of capital as money, bank drafts and documents (the shadow) or as the physical goods, machinery, etc., that follow (the substance). It doesn't matter which you visualize as capital. That is what the emigrant brings.

But I have tried to show that the days of single-man immigration are over. Even with a free homestead an immigrant can't come 'on his own'. He only clogs the labour market. The homestead days are gone by.

Our great need now is organized immigration. I think that it would restore our prosperity—as if we struck the granite rock of hard times and out of it flowed the pure waters of salvation.

I have already discussed the simpler and smaller organization of memorial settlement,—of people who come with money. I now turn to talk of the people who come with *none*. For these I propose to return to the principle of land company settle · ment which had such admirable results in old days in Upper Canada, and which was all too lightly laid aside. It would take a whole book to develop properly the subject of Land Settlement as a Company Enterprise. The best that one can hope to do here is to indicate the main purpose, and show the chief difficulties. We learn more by discussing and facing what's wrong with a plan than by dwelling on what's right with it.

Company settlement means a plan whereby a group of immigrants, in the course of a few consecutive years, are placed on a tract of land as a sort of going concern. The motive for it has to be found in a mixture of philanthropy and rapacity, the truly human half-and-half tonic. Men are not all greed, nor all goodness. To invite people to subscribe money for Empire Settlement Schemes, from which they get nothing themselves, will never carry far. The sources of such generosity are easily choked by the sands of difficulty and dispute. On the other hand any scheme for 'making a pile', for getting the last cent out of the immigrant and chiselling the last dollar of subsidy out of the government will only end in political scandal and disaster. Something in between is needed. Show me a company by which I can get five or six per cent. and also sit in a white robe with a harp, and I'm in on it. Such were the canny motives of old John Galt: and such, in a higher degree and with a greater illumination, the motives of Prince Rupert and his associates in founding that profitable and patriotic enterprise the Hudson's Bay Company.

Similarly Land Settlement must avoid the two extremes of naked individualism and hug-me-tight communism. The days are gone when you can settle a country by dumping down on it a rugged individual' with an axe and a dipper of whiskey. The days have not come when you can make a communist settlement with the work all allotted by the bosses, the food divided up by the assessors and the wives distributed by the Matrimonial Bureau. Communism sees no difficulty in Land Settlement; certainly not; if communism would work for society in general, the settlement of new land would be only one particular case. The greater would include the less.

In other words, in a successful company settlement the individual must be as far as possible 'on his own': not of necessity at once and in every case the owner of his own house, but at least the owner of his own wages. The company is a kind of frame in which individual fortune is fitted into a composite picture.

The feature of the situation which our generation has learned and which the previous one did not know, is the danger of collapse from falling prices and unsaleable products. To place a settlement of people principally to grow wheat, or to grow fruit, or to catch fish,—any sole or dominant occupation,—would mean inevitable shipwreck in the next price collapse. The bulwark against this lies in self-sufficiency, carried as far as ever it can be. The ideal settlement raises its own food and eats it: catches its own fish and cooks it; cuts its own lumber and builds its houses with it. It cooks, bakes, boils, cans, distills, ferments, sews, stitches, paints; it carpenters, it blacksmiths,—it pushes self-sufficiency as far as ever it can till the points where it meets the need for machine products from outside. These grudgingly it must buy, with things which, grudgingly, it will sell. Thus it can't print. It must buy *books*. But, after all, people never die for want of them. It can't sing: it may listen to a radio: but even Queen Victoria lived and died without one. The basic idea is that hard times will sweep away luxuries. But the rock bottom economic basis of life will still hold.

Thus in Company Settlement one would never make such calculations as that it costs more to can fruit than to buy it canned, more to raise hens than to buy eggs, more to raise hogs than to import hogs. All those fatal pieces of arithmetic have a trick in them. They take for granted something you *sell* in order to buy the outside stuff, and they take for granted the price you get. By this sin fell the Prairies. The unit size of land settlement is settled by certain obvious needs. It must be big enough for schools, including a high school. It cannot be big enough for a college. It must be big enough for a hospital; not for a medical school. It must have enough people to be able to use the machinery of lower manufacture: big enough for a planing mill, for a tannery, a brick yard (or several of each), not big enough to make paper but big enough to make houses. It must be big enough for farms, fields, pastures, woods, waters, hunting grounds and golf courses. It would work out at something like half the size of an Ontario county, say, 1,000 square miles,—a little over thirty miles each way. It would carry a population, in this stage of development, of two or three thousand people. Closer settlement would involve a different industrial regime only for favoured spots, and would come after.

The Land Settlement Company could expect to get in its charter from the government terms something of the sort that the Canada Company had, or the Wakefield Colonization Society in New Zealand. One may imagine a free grant of land: a certain amount of tax-exemption, initial or permanent for the shares and property: certain aid in making transportation facilities from where existing ones end to which their settlement block lies: this might mean a branch line railway: but more likely a truck road is good enough: erection at the cost of the Dominion of a post office and Federal buildings and presumably a gift of police protection. There is no trouble here except in details.

The company raises money as follows. A few people put up enough money for initial survey, search and negotiations. For what they spend thus they get presently extra shares. This has been done hundreds of times. The company, definitely organized after this, takes up subscriptions on shares. The appeal is patriotic as well as pecuniary. The company is pledged to bring out so many settlers a year, all British. The Charter allows a bond issue. It allows (This is doubtful ground) a dividend payment out of assets, at say 4 per cent. Not that this is vital but it induces people to come in.

With the money raised the Company 'engages' the immigrants. They go with wives, children and all, passage paid, everything paid. When they arrive in the Valley of Hope, they work for *wages*: they get part in cash, till they repay their passage money. Then they get *all* in cash, unless and until they want to take a holding, that is, to call their house their own, or take a blacksmith shop or any single enterprise. If they want to do that then they can, while still working for the company, leave a part of their wages to go as instalment against their tenure. It is the plan of the Irish Land Purchase of 1902 and of a hundred and one house-owning plans.

The company has marked out the Valley of Hope, not exactly into town lots, as now-a-days, but on a plan. Towns, we are told, are very soon (I mean in fifty years) going to give way to another form of human occupation of the land,—'centifrugal settlement' a sort of centre and suburbs,—everything trying to get away from the centre and seek space and isolation. In the Valley of Hope, just where the River of Peace joins its twin stream the River of Contentment, there will be an obviously central spot for Administration buildings, the Government buildings of Canada, the Hospital, the High School,—a *town* but with everything trying not to be in it.

There will be other focus points or lesser settlement. All this will be marked out ahead.

The company will mark and *keep* in reserve a lot of sites and locations. On others it will build houses, farmsteads, sawmills, and blacksmith shops, and carpenter shops,—At first the company does it all: then less and less: in about fifty years it winds up,—with a maximum set and a minimum hoped for, as the final compensation of its shareholders.

One asks what are the *receipts* of the company? In cash very little at first, hardly anything. Very likely there is something which it can produce with its hired labour and sell, even at the start. But the process would be risky and should be kept carefully in control. What it would sell would depend on the location: it might be lumber or pulp-wood or fish, or in limits and carefully, grain and fruit.

But every time the company builds a house, or builds a dam, an asset is created, though no cash return appears as yet. That is why it is allowed to pay a dividend out of capital. One asks why pay a dividend at all? The reason is psychological. People will subscribe ever so much more readily if there is an actual dividend than even for a far larger dividend in prospect.

But company's cash receipts will grow all the time. Outside services, not part of the life-tissue of the land settlement, will pay a revenue. Thus,— the company builds a moving picture theatre at Hope Centre and an outsider rents it and puts on films: he also rents a house to live in. The picture house and the picture man are non-essential. In hard times they must look out for themselves. So is the barber who opens the shop and gives Roman Massage to the blacksmith. He is not a company man. He pays rent and if hard times come, and it's a close shave, then he'll have to make it a little closer.

Very soon a large group of non-essential outsiders will attach to the settlement. They are like tissue turning into bone. One asks who pays them? The answer is that they partly pay one another as when the barber goes to moving pictures and the moving picture man gets shaved, and both pay the company rent to do it. Also the company's own people from the start have money,—

real money, not scrip, not prosperity,—paid to them as whole or part wages.

Other revenues keep coming. The company permits 'Manorial Settlement' for people arriving with their own money to take up a 'Manor'. This brings in the money for building and the money for the land.

But turn a moment to the difficulties and watch how they multiply like a cloud of flies. I remember how once a distinguished college principal under whom I served said, "When I hear of a new scheme being advocated I never ask who's for it but *who's against it*". So it is well to see what a lot of difficulties there are. Where do these Pilgrims of Hope get medical service? Private practice wouldn't do, obviously,—it would mean no doctors or too many doctors. State doctors,— that is, hired by the company? But one knows all the present difficulty with that in England and in the British Columbia scheme.—I think a modified system, company doctors and a company hospital, but with a private supplemental fee to keep the advantage of private-practice.

School teachers? Does the provincial school system apply, or does the company do it all? I don't know.

Liquor. How much do they drink and where do they get it. I don't know. But they'll get it somehow.

Much more difficult problem,—the Mail Order List. *Must* the Pilgrims of Hope buy their boots from the local bootmaker, made with local leather? Can't they order from outside? I'm just afraid they can't, not the essential things, made in the Valley,—no. Then can the boot-maker charge what he pleases? and if not, isn't that getting close to socialism? Well it does look like it. . . . And yet certain self-sufficient trades *must* be kept up. . . . Better go and think about it some more.

Electric light? I guess they can't have it. Plumbing? I think that can be local.

Turn to some of the easy things. For example, hotels,—will there be hotels? Ah! Will there! That'll be one of the best things the company does and from which it draws a real revenue. There will be more 'tourists' coming to look at the new settlement than can be found beds for. They'll have to stay awake all night and spend money.

The company management? Does that imply a set of angels as it does under socialisim? I don't think so. I think that ordinary company manage-ment would apply to the Valley of Hope. Of-ficials nominated by the Directors, and paid and retained according to results, would meet the needs of the case. Results would be judged, presum-ably, not solely and brutally in terms of last-cent profit. It would include the idea of social con-tentment, of human happiness. Success or failure would soon write itself all over the Valley and good management would prove itself, bad man-agement condemn itself.

*   *   *   *   *

The great merit of a plan of Company Settlement, on some such lines as indicated, is that if it succeeds once, it can de done again. It can be duplicated over and over. It is, in other words, if it succeeds, an invention. After that, we know how. Vainly have people sought in the past for such single-type inventions of social organization, which once successful spread of their own power. Such was Fourier's dream of his 'Phalaux', so widely heralded a century ago. Such was Louis Blanc's famous National Workshops of the France of 1848. Those failed. Perhaps this wont.

* * * * *

It's a beautiful dream anyway. And I don't see why, worked out in more careful detail, it should not enlist support.

CHAPTER FIFTEEN

THE LAND OF DREAMS

The North Beyond the Provinces: Its Vast
Extent and Inspiration: The Great Company:
Arm Chair Exploration of the Arctic: My
Fellow Explorers — Franklin, Amundsen,
Bernier, Stefannson and Shackleton: Our
Trusteeship of the North.

Nearly half of Canada lies outside of the provinces and to the north of them,—a land area of
1,500,000 square miles out of 3,500,000. This
is made up of the Yukon, between the Rockies
and Alberta; the Mackenzie District between Al-
berta-Saskatchewan and the Polar Sea; Keewatin,
chiefly the 'barren lands' between Manitoba, the
Hudson Bay and the Polar Sea; and Franklin, the
vast territory of broken islands reaching to an
apex at the pole. It is, in point of human life
an empty country,—in all 14,000 people on an
extent of land equal to that in which 300,000,000
souls live, or try to, in British India: emptier still
as far as white people go, there being 2,500 in the
Yukon and about a thousand in the Territories.

But it is far from empty in its resources, its
future, and in its inspiration. The great forests
of Canada reach away beyond the sixtieth parallel:
they carry a frontier line that lies in a north-west
slant from Fort Churchill to Great Bear Lake. In
the Mackenzie basin there are still plenty of big
spruce trees of 100 feet height and of a diameter
up to eighteen inches. A last skirmish line of

stunted spruce and scrub willow reaches to the
Arctic Sea itself, at the mouths of the Mackenzie
Delta. In the Mackenzie District local lumber
suffices for all needs of building. The mineral
wealth of the Yukon, in this new age of metals,
may at any time restore the lost glory of Dawson
City and its fellow camps. The reindeer just
introduced into the Arctic grazing lands, may soon
rival the herd of 700,000 now feeding in Alaska,
where none existed a generation ago. Our far
North has pasture, so says the Porsild report
of 1928, for at least three quarters of a million
animals.

The furs from the Territories, chiefly from
Mackenzie, number about 250,000 skins a year
with muskrat as the chief item, and about 7,000
beaver and 11,000 white fox, a total value running from a million to a million and a half dollars.

The Mackenzie District, if not a land flowing
with milk and honey, at least flows with petroleum
and natural gas. The secret store of radium in the
rocks of the Great Bear Lake may make Croesus
of Lydia look poverty-stricken. The district has
already a steam boat commerce that covers 1,300
miles of navigation. The aeroplane is as familiar
a sight to the native Indian as a bus to a Cockney.
Even the 'barren lands' carpeted with flowers
blush with red copper.

*   *   *   *   *

But to me this far away north suggests not
modern commerce, but a land of dreams, of infinite horizons, of blue, blue sky and of bright

sunshine on the snow, more invigorating than
warmth itself. Such dreams carry back to the far
away days when first the ships of the Hudson's
Bay Company sailed into the waters of the mid-
night sun.

*   *   *   *   *

Some years ago I was engaged in Montreal in
what is called 'historical research', a thing done
by professors in the heart of the summer in the
depth of a library where there is no one to check
up their time. Often it takes years and years to
write a chapter.

But the point is that I wanted to make a reference to the foundation of the Hudson's Bay Company over two and a half centuries ago, and I
wanted to be certain of their official name. The
companies of those days had queer names. all
alike and yet all different—'gentlemen' of this
and 'adventurers' of that, or 'merchants' of the
other. I couldn't remember whether the Hudson's
Bay Company were called gentlemen, or adventurers, or business men, or captains of industry, or
crooks. I looked into a lot of old volumes and got
no wiser. Then a sudden idea came to me: "I'll
telephone them!" It had occurred to my mind
that the Hudson's Bay Company of Charles the
Second were still right there down town in Montreal and doing business. So I called the number
and asked, "Would you mind telling me the full
official name of your company?" "Certainly.
We're often asked for it. We're the Governor

and Company of Adventurers of England trading into Hudson's Bay."

It seems wonderful, doesn't it? I almost
imagined myself going a little further and saying,
"Hullo, Prince Rupert, can I speak with your
cousin Mr. Charles the Second?" "Hold the line
a minute and I'll see. I'm sorry, our Mr. Charles
is in conference with our Miss Nell Gwynne, and
we don't like to disturb him."

                *   *   *   *   *

The thoughts aroused by such an incident
characterize the size and majesty of the Great
North; the fascinating sweep of time and space
that its name involves; the North, where man
scribbles in vain a little history and Nature buries
it in a blizzard of snow.

The North is the only place where Nature still
can claim to rule, the only place as yet but little
vexed by man. All over the globe there spreads
his noisy failures; the North alone is silent and in
peace. Give man time and he will spoil that too;
but the time has not, thank Heaven, as yet arrived. The fascists, we read, are mowing down the
reds, or the yellows, or whatever they are, in
Barcelona with machine guns. But the Eskimos
of Ungava are not troubling the Algonquins.
Someone is dropping bombs all round Gibraltar,
but none fall on the delta of the Mackenzie. The
organization of the air defence of London hums as
loud as the mosquitoes of the Great Slave Lake,
but all is quiet on the Coppermine. The Poles
are so worked up about their corridor to the sea

that there may be a first class war about it; but the
Indians are using the same old portage route from
the Moose to the Albany, and going right across
the railway track, and no one worries about it.

Compared with the rest of a troubled world, the
North seems a vast realm of peace.

*   *   *   *   *

No great war, no war on a real scale, ever devas-
tated the great northwest. But listen to this forgotten——or rather unknown——episode of history.
That arch-disturber of mankind, Napoleon Bona-
parte, once tried to make such a war, once planned
to strike at England by means of a great sweep to
be made from the snow-covered plains and mountains of the West. This was to take the Canadas
and the settlements of the seaboard from the rear.
Students of military science like myself (I like
it best when it's about a hundred and fifty years
old) do not need to be told that a crack in the
rear is about the most deadly thing that one
general can administer to the other. That is why
a great commander like Marlborough or Napoleon
was always careful to have his rear resting on
something reliable——like a marsh, or broken rock
or a field of cactus. And that was why a great
mind like that of Napolean would turn to
grandiose schemes of hitting, not merely another
general in the rear, but a whole nation. Napoleon
went to Egypt, not to kill the Egyptians——that
was just done on the side——but with a view to getting at the rear of Turkey, and he planned the still
vaster enterprise of throwing India on the rear of

Europe. But for the defeat of Tippoo Sahib at
Seringapatam this might have been done. Read-
ers who don't know about this 'rear' business
often wonder how people like Tippoo Sahib and
Zenghis Khan get into our history. That's it—
by the rear entrance.

Well, at any rate Napoleon's plan was to organize the vast tribes of the Northwest—presumably the Crees and the Doukhobors and the Al-
bertans—to overwhelm Ottawa and Montreal.
His idea was correct in a way and came true later
on, but it was premature. It was characteristic
of Napoleon's profound ignorance of America, to
imagine the Northwest filled with likely looking
Indians who could be recruited into Kellerman's
dragoons and Milhaud's cuirassiers and descend
(in four or five days) from the Rocky Mountains
on Montreal with cries of 'Vive l'Empereur!'

So Napoleon set out to get information. All
that could be found out in Paris (the year was
about 1805) was that a man called Mackenzie
had been right across the continent to the Pacific
Ocean and had written a book about it, published in 1801 under the title "Voyages on the
River St. Lawrence and Through the Continent
of America to the Frozen and Pacific Oceans"—
which, for a Scotchman, was short and snappy.
Napoleon ordered the book translated in French
and printed. Only two or three copies were
made, beautifully bound and embellished. There
is no trace of any of them left except of the copy
given to General Bernadotte, afterwards, by

Napoleon's influence, made Crown Prince of Sweden, and great-grandfather to the present King. Napoleon wrote to Bernadotte about the scheme, and hence our knowledge of it. The information gathered showed its emptiness—at the time—but later on the notion of a descent from Alberta to take Ottawa in the rear has been worked out with success.

When I write about the North I speak with a certain authority. For I know the North, as few people know it. In the corporeal, bodily sense, I have never been there. But in my arm chair, in front of the fire in my house on Cote des Neiges Road in Montreal, I have traversed it all, from the portages back of Lake Superior to where the Mackenzie delta washes into the tidal seas. I have been with Franklin on the Coppermine and Coronation Gulf, with Hudson till I lost him owing to his own folly, with Mackenzie over the divide, in Red River ox-carts with Butler, and in the foothills with Milton and Cheadle. In the snow-storms and Arctic blizzards I feel perfectly at home; if it gets really bad I just lie down in the snow, along with Stefansson, and let it bury me completely and lie there for a day or two and read a book till it moderates. But I must say I don't think I ever felt such intense cold as on crossing the Coppermine running hard with ice through barren treeless country of slate and stone. Imagine trusting oneself on a river like that on a sort of raft or boat made of willow sticks, wet to the skin, in piercing cold. I had to get up and mix a hot

whisky and stir the fire and leave Franklin and
Richardson to freeze awhile till I rejoined them.
A fine story that, "The Journey to the Polar Sea,"
by John Franklin: not the narrative of his im-
mortal adventure and heroic death, but the earlier
journey down the Mackenzie and along the polar
shores with Richardson and young Back.   There
is a very human little incident in the tale of how
Lieutenant Back, youthful and ardent, nearly got
left out of the expedition—stayed behind to go
to a dance.   They sailed without him and he
caught them at the Orkneys or somewhere.   Back
later became a knight and an admiral, returned to
the North, again as an explorer, and discovered
the Back river, not the one at Montreal but the
one that commemorates his name.

Let no one think, from what was said above, of
the silence and peace of the North that I am trying
to depict it as a vast frozen emptiness.   Far be it
from me to fall into that worn-out fallacy of the
lifelessness of the North.   If I ever shared it, I was
cured of it long ago by an angry letter I once received from Vilhjalmar Stefansson, an angry letter
that proved the beginning of a personal friendship
of over twenty years.   I had written a little book
called "The Adventures of the Far North," and
had spoken in it of the North as if "Here in this
vast territory civilization has no part and life no
place.   Life struggles northward only to die out
in the Arctic cold."

Stefansson, who takes a personal pride in the
North and regards Baffin Bay as a superior social

centre to Naragansett Beach, felt affronted and wrote, in substance: "You may be a h—— of a humorist, but what you don't know about the North would fill a book. Don't you understand that the North is full of flowers and butterflies and life everywhere?" I answered back mildly: "I meant further north still. The thing must stop somewhere." But I learned the lesson, and I know now that it is just a poet's fancy to speak of the Great North as 'silent and untenanted.' I am well aware, without being told again by Tyrrel or Stefansson, or anyone touchy about it, that the north "teems everywhere with animal and plant life." I read the other day a rather spiteful account, by an English settler, of the mosquitoes on the shores of the Great Slave Lake that made me quite envious. I happen to be the president of the Anti-Mosquito Society of East Simcoe, one of the few active offices that I still retain in retirement. What with coal oil and such things, we have killed off so many mosquitoes that we are beginning to run out of them and may have to send for more. It is good to know that if a real shortage comes the Great Slave lake district can supply an adequate 'carryover'.

But if the North, even at its emptiest, still waves with Arctic flowers and hums with a mist of insects, there is a sense in it which contrasts with all other parts of the globe. The role of man and nature, as seen elsewhere, are reversed. The elemental forces still rule; and over it falls, inevitable and eternal, the winter night.

Vilhjalmar Stefansson is not the only one of the great explorers of our time whom I have been privileged to know. I recall a wonderful evening in my home at Montreal, listening to Raoul Amundsen, just back from his discovery of the South Pole. The eminence of that exploit makes it part of the history of the world, and makes people lose from sight Amundsen's earlier achievement: his accomplishment, in the little *Gjoa,* of the north-west passage, which gives him a place in the heroic annals of Canada. Amundsen, when I met him, was lecturing—a job which he hated as much as all good lecturers do—in order to get enough money to make another polar voyage, anywhere so long as it was polar. I was to be chairman of his meeting, and so I called upon him after breakfast with a list of social invitations—things he abominated. I said, "Captain Amundsen, the Ladies' Morning Musical would like to invite you as their guest this morning." "Thank you," he said, "but I would rather not." I went on to the next item. "Sir William Peterson would like to know if you would care to come up at ten o'clock and see McGill University?" "Thank you; I would rather not see it." "The Women's Canadian Club are holding a lunch and would like you to come as a guest of honour." "That is very kind, but I would rather not." "The Ski Club want to give a tea." "No, thank you." "The Norski Danski, and Svenski Associations would like to escort you with torches from the hotel to the hall." "It is very kind, but no, I would rather take a cab."

"Now," I said, "we come to the last item. After your lecture is over, will you come up to my house and have some Scotch whiskey?" "Yes, very gladly, indeed; that is most kind." And at my house that night Amundsen talked till the small hours of his South Pole experience, talking chiefly with Jack McCrae of Flanders Fields, who was also a polar explorer of sorts, having just made a trip through the Hudson Straits.

I also knew Captain Bernier, our own Canadian explorer, who saw more of our arctic seas than any other living man. I met him at a big dinner in New York, where he was the chief guest. He had some moving pictures—very new and very imperfect things then—of polar scenes. Bernier apologized for them. "I 'ave to hapologize," he said, "for the pictures. We didn't know ver' well how to take them. This one is call' 'Heskimo Loading Coal'!"

Load it they certainly did! The picture had been taken with a wrong timing; the Eskimos dashed in one hop a hundred yards from the ship to a great cliff of coal; their picks moved so fast you could not see the points; they filled bags of coal in four seconds; and were back on the ship in one hop. Next to me at the banquet sat an American coal man. "Gee," he said, "I wish I had those fellers at thirty cents an hour!"

Ernest Shackleton I knew also, and well. It is not generally known, for it has never been made history, that after the war Shackleton planned a Canadian polar expedition to explore the Beaufort Sea. He had wanted to go south again, but the British admiralty were very half-hearted about giving him support. So he turned to Canada, and came to Montreal to raise money. I was one of those who tried to help in this, and, with the government's and private generosity, we soon had plenty of money in sight for the expedition. Exploration is as cheap as human life itself. I arranged on behalf of Shackleton for the services of a corps of young McGill scientists. Then he asked me if I would like to go as historiographer, and I said yes. I knew McGill would spare me. Any college would send its staff to the Beaufort Sea any time. I said I needed no pay, and so for twenty-four hours I was historiographer of the Beaufort Sea Canadian Expedition.

But it came to a sudden end. I said to Shackleton that I would supply all my own Scotch whiskey for the year's trip, as I didn't want to be a charge on the ship. And he said they didn't take whiskey on polar expeditions and, outside of the medicine chest, didn't allow it. Another illusion of the North shattered! I always thought that explorers, the ship once well set in the ice and buried in snow, went down below with a pack of cards and a keg of whiskey. But it seems not. They take observations. I resigned, and a little later news came that the admiralty had gone right about face and Shackleton was given a ship, and he went south and never came back.

But all of this that I have said of the North is supposed to move gropingly towards a general idea, to throw a dim light upon a general conclusion.   Here is this vast, beautiful space—the last part of human heritage to be reached and explored by man.   Not much longer can it remain in isolation.   Its infinite distance is gone.   It thrills with the waves and currents of talking voices: over it hovers the searching aeroplane.   Mankind has taken the empty savannahs of the West and is moving on the North.   Human life and human livelihood have learned easily to adapt themselves where once was hyperborean darkness.

We, speaking collectively for all mankind, have for the present at least made a mess of the rest of the world.   Our contriving wits and calculating selfishness had somehow cheated us of what seemed our inheritance.   Man struggles in the grasp of his own machinery.

For the North let us make it different.   If the vast lands that edge the polar seas—Scandinavia, Russia, Canada—are to be filled with electric light that dims the aurora, with power that defies the cold, and resources that supply the world, let us see to it that in the new trust of the future of the North we make fewer errors than in the old.

CHAPTER SIXTEEN
WAYS AND MEANS OF SALVATION

Public Opinion — Youth — Constitutional Amendment—Consolidation of Debt—Railway Unification—Dominion Economic Control—Immigration—Development of Resources.

In all institutions, in all laws, the inspiring spirit must come first. Legislation is worthless except as it expresses a purpose already there. People cannot be made virtuous by act of parliament, honest by an order-in-council, or sober by a municipal by-law. It is the fault of younger people, especially of academic people, to think that society can be made and fashioned by law. It is part of the very innocence of their optimism. Laws merely express and make regular the forces that the mind and will of society have already brought into being. It is because people are determined not to steal that we have laws against burglary. The burglar is the odd man out. He is the exception that proves the rule.

What we need to do, therefore, in Canada for our salvation is, first of all, to renew a right heart and spirit within us. We need first of all an ardent purpose to make things better.

I do not think that this can be done by intensifying party politics. The organization and play of parties is perhaps necessary in operating the institutions under which we live. It makes government possible, by creating an artificial union and subordinating the fool to the wiser

255

man. But it is, after all, pretty much of a Punch
and Judy show. We ought, as far as we can, to
temper it with reality, as every great national
crisis automatically does. Yet even with parties
still as our means of practical government we can
do much. Every political party that enlists and
keeps the sympathy and support of thousands of
decent followers, must have good in it. This
good becomes evident as history flows on, and
shows it like the grains of gold in the bed of the
moving river.

So it is with us.

I wish that for our welfare we could combine
those elements which have chiefly distinguished
each of our political parties: the empire patriotism
of the Conservative, the stubborn honesty of the
Liberal, the optimism of the Socialist, the driving
power of the Social Crediter, and the unsullied
enthusiasm of all who write on their banner the
name and the inspiration of youth.

We older people are a damaged lot. We lived
at the wrong time to be of full use now. Our
youth was in the hey-day of democracy and peace,
undreaming of social catastrophe. Politics was a
form of career, a game. It was smart to be crooked
and get away with it. Ward politicians with
diamond necktie pins, Ottawa 'members' with
silk hats, slick and rich out of nothing,—these
people gave us a false lead. They made government seem as slick as themselves, a 'cinch' not a
sacrifice. It didn't matter much then. It does

now. We must change it. We must have men 'whose hearts are in the cause'.

To get them we must appeal to youth, to the rising generation. We must revive the idea of government as a sacred trust, public dishonesty as dirty sin. Young people are capable of this.

One sees here and there in a world arising out of its past distress to newer efforts this movement of ideal youth. It is no new thing. It is as old as youth itself. Its history is written in a hundred wars of liberation. We need it now for the liberation of peace.

I wish we could take a few smart men and hang them.

* * * * *

To turn then from the ground of idealism and purpose, without which we stand on shifting sand, it can be asked what are the plain and simple measures which such a purpose can direct.

I set them down here in summary as I have tried to indicate them in this book.

We need, first, a method of amending our constitution by a general vote, as in Australia and other places. We need to use amendment to restore central economic power to the Dominion.

We need to do away with *ultra vires* and *intra vires* decisions in regard to Dominion economic legislation. We should indicate what field the Dominion should cover and then let every Dominion Act be a good one, as is now every British Act. Lawyers might take fright at this self-interpretative power.   Logically it equals depotism, but logic is seldom as good as horse-sense.

We need to relieve our debt by consolidating it. If we institute one general debt, guaranteed by the Dominion and all the provinces, each with a pro rata allotment of it to wipe out all or part of its present debt, we can float it at $2\frac{1}{2}$ per cent. No loan council is needed.   We allocate specific revenue from each province.   This was the old Turkish method: the Sultan used no other: that is, no one would lend him money on any other. That shows how good the method is.

We should then settle our present railway muddle, make it all government or all company.

The president of the Canadian Pacific is quoted in a recent American magazine as saying that our failure to unify the railway system costs us "an economic wastage of from fifty to seventy-five million dollars a year."   It is true that he is quoted not in his own direct voice but "as told to William Holmes".   But that's all right.   All the great people, like Napoleon and Abraham Lincoln and the Queen of Sheba, speak through a medium. It's expensive and that's why Napoleon costs a dollar-fifty, but it has a personal touch.   And anyone who has followed the courageous and untiring efforts of the President of the Canadian Pacific to arouse the people of Canada against the muddle and the menace of our railway situation, will know the weight that attaches to a personal statement from him.   Yet so far he has been only *vox clamantis in eremis,* which is the Latin for a broadcast in Saskatchewan.

If the railway is to be all government, let it have all the money it likes.   What it loses we gain. The man who rides most on the cars and ships most freight wins out.   But there's something in it for everybody, as the electrician said to the criminal.   Or else we can make it all one company, with dividends limited and rates controlled.   But *unify* we must.   A man can't limp forever.   A dog can't always run on three legs.   A country can't go forward and drag a ball and chain like the present.   These things being done, we should open the country up, capital and immigrants in floods—ships, colonies, commerce,—part of a world wide British system such as our grandfathers dreamed of,—in other words, be an empire.

CHAPTER SEVENTEEN

NO VOTE OF THANKS

The Chairman Winds Me Up—I Vote the
Thanks Myself—Rah! Rah! College—My Old
Students—The Dean and the Dropping Pin—
The Lady and the Loud Speaker—My Dis-
covery Ends.

In writing this book I have been so interested
in the subjects of the chapters that I have said less
and less about my lectures. But as a matter of
fact they were going on all the time. At the
beginning of each lecture the chairman still said,
"Professor Leacock needs no introduction." And
at the end he said, "I am sure, ladies and gentlemen, that the speaker needs no formal vote of
thanks." So I never got that either.

But I didn't need it. The warmth of my reception spoke of itself. That's the great thing
about the Prairies, the colder it is outside, the
warmer it is in the human heart. Don't talk to
me of languid audiences in the tropics, sticky
with heat and faint with saturation. You
couldn't knock a laugh out of them with a
hockey stick. But let me have the Quota Club of
Medicine Hat, or the Wives and Mothers of
Regina, or the Old Boys of Anything (a pretty
young crowd) at Edmonton or Saskatoon,—with
20 to 30 below outside and the snow against the
hotel windows!—and you've a grand start towards a big evening if you don't spoil it yourself.
Then let someone hit up the harmonium and let

everybody ask the world to "give me a home where
the antelope roam and the buffalo wander at
will." Have the chairman say, "Mr. Leacock does
not need,—" of course not—and you're off.

It was very strange for me, going through the
West. It seemed like a world of lost memories.
As I said in a chapter above, my recollections of
hearing about the West of fifty years ago when
my father and uncle and older brothers went there,
made me seem to know it without having been
there.

When I heard the Quota Club ask for a home
"where the antelope roam", the song came back
to me from fifty years before. I had never heard
it in between. My brother Dick served in the
Mounted Police. He joined at Regina along with
the late Lieut.-Governor Primrose in 1885-6.
When he came back on 'furlough', after three
years, he brought with him a banjo on which he
played what he understood to be 'chords'. I remember that he sang for us to give him "a home
where the antelope roam": and my mother said,
that summer evening, that she wished some one
would give it to him.

Dick has a home now, a quiet one,—he's had
it these fourteen years. But, as with many another
dispossessed child of the West that we failed to
develop, his home is out beyond the clatter of an
American industrial city and not where "the
prairie flower blows softly and the scented rose-
bud trains its wealth of summer beauty o'er the
riders of the plains." We should see to it that

the next wave of settlers in the West can at least find graves there.

*   *   *   *   *

But it was not merely my own family recollections that made the West to me a sort of retrospect. It was the number of people whom I met again there whom I hadn't seen, had lost from memory for a generation, or, to put it more widely, who had been lost for a generation from the sight and immediate memory of the crowd who were once their close friends at school or college. They went away. We lost track of them; young men don't write letters. So we would casually ask, "What became of so-and-so?" "He went to Moose Jaw" or "He went to Revelstoke." That was the end of him. Most characteristic of all: "He went to the Klondyke." That was the borne from which no traveller returned.

It was strange to find that a lot of them were still there, just where they had gone to: that 'Spot' who had 'gone to Moose Jaw' thirty years ago was still in Moose Jaw: after all why not? He was an honour mathematician. Where could he go? It was strange to find that 'Herbie' who went to the Klondyke, in 1897, had come back; he was an amateur ventriloquist and conjurer: we thought of course that the Indians got him: but he was back, a war-colonel in Vancouver, still conjuring. Old indeed they looked: especially at first sight, old and furrowed and not hair enough on half a dozen of them for one rugby-football player of the '90's. But as you looked at them their faces changed back to shape again, the lines faded out, and with a drink or two, even their hair came back.

Old of course: for my own sixty-seventh birthday fell in when I was at Victoria on December 30, 1936.

It is amazing how the years slip away. I had got old and hadn't noticed it. And, of course, there is always the regret for the wasted time, the things that one might have done.

Look at the Emperor Charles the Fifth of Spain; long before he was my age he had ruled over half Europe and retired into a monastery to pray, and I haven't even started; and George III! At my age he'd been crazy twice, and had got over it. I haven't.

Someone in Vancouver said to me that it made him feel old to think that so many of his friends are dead. I told him I had got past that. I am old enough to expect them to be dead and they keep getting resurrected. My trouble is resurrection. They suddenly appear in clubs and hotels and say, "Don't you know me?" and I answer, "Go away; dematerialize yourself; don't haunt me."

I am sure that lots of other men of my age suffer from these cases of premature resurrection. Some of them peculiarly distressing. I recall the incident of my old friend Boygate of Montreal. I am sure he won't mind, I mean wouldn't have minded, my mentioning his name thus in print. I came into my Club one afternoon (the University Club, next door to McGill University, Quebec License), and it suddenly occurred to me how greatly I missed Boygate now that he was gone: I wished that while he was still with us, I had seen more of him, had taken more occasion to sit with him round the Club, of which he, like myself, was a charter member. I realized that I had always been too self-centred, too much in a hurry to break away, had all too little appreciated the company of my friends. Ah, well, too late to change now! And just while I was feeling these regrets, in he walked! "Boygate!" I exclaimed, shaking hands warmly while my eyes almost filled with tears. To think of it! Here he was alive again, either resurrected or never dead, it didn't matter which. "Hullo! hullo!" he said warmly in return, "come on up to the lounge and let's sit and have a talk." "Boygate," I said, looking at my watch, as the world of customary habit closed round me, "I'm sorry! I have to rush off to a meeting,—another time, eh?"

So what was the use of his resurrection after all. Life is like that. It's well they don't come back.

But mentioning my University, where I worked so long (thirty-five years) reminds me of one pleasant feature of my lecture tour. My old students! There they were all over the West, in every town,—waiting for me, in some cases I was told, laying for me. But in any case they were there. Not so many graduates perhaps from the faculty of Liberal Arts: Arts men find it harder to get work in the West now that there are

so few livery stables.   But men of the other facul-
ties everywhere.

I struck, however, one or two perplexing cases
of the identity of former students.   Thus at Fort
William, at the very beginning of my lecture tour,
the barber who cut my hair called me "Professor".
He said, "I'll trim it a little full over the ear, eh,
Professor?"   And I said, "Yes, either that or trim
the ear."   Then noticing that he called me "Professor", I said, "Are you from McGill?"   He
answered, "Yes, sir, I left in 1913, came right here
to Fort William, got a chair here in six months
and have done fine ever since!   Two other boys
came on the same train and have chairs down the
street!"   That looked fine as academic advance-
ment, three appointments to chairs in one and
the same town!   But afterwards, I didn't feel so
sure, my ears were pretty well shrouded with
towels.   He may have said, "Montreal" and not
McGill.   Anyway, he and the other two boys, he
says, are going back for a vacation "to see the old
place", some day, so one can watch for them and
see where they go.

I had the pleasure of addressing a good many
groups of McGill graduates either at dinners
specially organized, or in conjunction with other
organizations; I had also the still greater pleasure
of meeting a lot of them personally in individual
fashion. In some places McGill graduates are as
thick as Milton's autumn leaves in Vallombrosa
(Saskatchewan), in other places rare as four-leaf
clovers.   But there are always a few: and they

stand everywhere high in social credit, except in Alberta, where they keep away from it. Relatively to its size, there are more McGill men in Regina—the headquarters of the Police—than anywhere else. This may be just old habit: it's hard to break with old associations.

Speaking in a general way one may say that in the West McGill predominates in medicine, Queen's in the Church and Toronto at (not behind) the Bar. Thus McGill attends the sick and when McGill medicine has done its work, Queen's buries them and when they're buried Toronto divides up their estates among the three. It is what Adam Smith so happily called the Division of Labour.

I must not presume to give a full account of the various meetings at which I was the chief figure— what they call in the London pantomime the Principal Boy. But I may say a word or two here of the character of some of the gatherings.

At the dinner at Port Arthur it was realized that there weren't enough graduates to go round. We made up a big dinner however by taking in graduates of Toronto, of Queen's and of various American colleges. At first in the dark you couldn't tell them apart. But presently you could see which were the Queen's men by the way they stood up at once for Grace while the McGill men were still asking 'What's the matter?' But when the drinks came round there was no doubt which was the senior college.

At Regina, which is as I say a great McGill

centre, we had a very grand dinner, heavily attended and roaring with enthusiasm.   I spoke, I remember, on *The Value of Imbecility in Education*.   It was more or less the same kind of talk that I had given at Port Arthur under the title *Our National Heritage*.   But I soon discovered and I recommend to others the proper method of composing a McGill speech.   Announce it in the press under some such title as *Spontaneous Idealism in Education*.   But when you speak, let the talk run something like this:

"Some of you, I suppose, can still recall dear old Dean Pat Johnson; let me tell you a story about *Pat* (Hoorah!) (Cheers) . . . . and before I touch on Idealism, gentlemen, I'd like to tell another story about King Cook, the janitor of the Medical Building (shouts of joy) . . . . Some of you—nearly all of you—recall Dean Moyse, Charlie Moyse!   (Applause! shouts! tears!. . . . Someone tries to start *Hail! Alma Mater*—but gets it too low) . . . . And before I sit down, gentlemen, I'd like to ask you to rise, if you can— and drink if you can still hold anything to old McGill—applause!—dear old McGill.   (Shouts —our Alma Mater.)

Next day the Regina paper said, "Professor Leacock's talk last night to the McGill graduates, a searching Analysis of Education (a subject entirely novel to them) was followed with rapt attention.   The chairman in thanking the professor said that he had never listened to anything like it before and anyway he hadn't listened to more than the first few sentences."

But at Edmonton it was the other way. The graduates seemed overwhelmingly to be all Toronto men. As I have the good luck to be a graduate of four different Canadian Universities, I am able to be all things to all men.

So we had, at the Macdonald Hotel, a very grand Varsity Dinner. I made the same speech as at the McGill Dinner in Regina, but I called it "Our Ocean Empire." I changed the text a little to make it run:

"I don't know how many of you present remember our old president Sir Daniel Wilson (Cheers—we do!)—We used to call him "Dan" (shouts—"we did")—and some of you recall Professor Chapman (Yes! Yes!) or perhaps I'd better just say Chappie (Hoorah!) .... At any rate I want to say that Old Varsity is just the same grand old college (Cheers and College Yells —V-A-R-S-I-T-Y).

*   *   *   *   *

I told a great many stories of old college days, at dinners and incidentally and *obiter*, but none that called forth kinder memory and warmer affection than my reminiscences of the lectures of a byegone and beloved Dean of Arts.

The Dean, as every one remembers, loved lecturing, in college and out of it. It was his life. And he never lectured with greater zest than when some local society invited him to deliver his famous lecture on Lichfield Cathedral. I always knew

when such a night was coming because the Dean
would spend that day busy over a huge map of
the cathedral, with compass and pointers, re-
measuring it. A real lecturer has a sense of re-
sponsibility. An error of the eighth of an inch
might queer the lecture. The next morning he
would come bustling into his office smiling and
rosy with his triumph of the night before. "How
did your lecture go, Mr. Dean?" I asked.
"Marvelous! simply marvelous! never gave a
better—or perhaps, if that's exaggerating—not
often. Everything just right—map up on the
wall—good light on it—hall almost dark—
lectured on, didn't notice the time, looked at my
watch—suddenly found I'd been lecturing an hour
and a half! 'Well, ladies and gentlemen,' I said,
'shall I go on?' not a sound! absolutely absorbed!
you could have heard a pin drop! lectured on
another hour and then said, "Well, I'm afraid I
must stop," and had the lights turned on! The
audience seemed just to start up into life—just
like out of a dream! I heard one man near me
say, 'Good God! has he finished?'" . . . .

With that the Dean rolled up Lichfield Cathedral and put it away for the next time. But I
used often to think how terrible it would have
been if some one had dropped a pin during his
lecture! What a crash!

Talking of stories to entertain an audience, I
told one several times in the West that seemed to
me amazingly funny, and all the more so because

it was literally and exactly true, and needed no alteration or embellishment.

I always told it as if it had happened a night or two before in a rival town. People like that best. Local jokes beat all others. In Orillia, where I live, we like a joke on Barrie; and in ancient Rome they enjoyed a crack at Carthage.

But as a matter of fact this incident happened in the Ladies' Club of a great American city, a beautiful new building, with all the equipment brand new, and a lovely auditorium with a brand new loud-speaker.

Before the meeting the lady-President said to me, "I must apologize for our loud-speaker. Don't mind if it starts to make queer noises. There's something wrong with it, but we don't just know what it is."

No, she didn't know, and I didn't know, and they didn't know what was wrong with it, but a little later we *all* knew. The trouble was that there were two plumbers in the basement under the platform trying to connect up a furnace.

So the lady-President in beginning the meeting said,—

"Ladies, before I introduce the speaker of to-day I want to say a few words of warning. Our loud-speaker was just installed and I'm afraid,"— and here she assumed a manner of charming apology,—"I'm afraid it isn't behaving itself very well" . . . .

At that moment the loud-speaker broke in with a giant voice,—

"Get something under her and lift her up,—
she's not working right."

There was a frozen silence, with ripples of
giggles breaking the ice.

The lady-President said,—

"Ladies, I'm afraid" . . . .

And the loud-speaker shouted,—

"Stick a crowbar under her and get a purchase
on her" . . . .

"Ladies, I must ask someone" . . . .

"She's full of ashes, heave her up and shake the
ashes out of her" . . . .

"Ladies, will someone please" . . . .

"It's her tubes,—they're not connected" . . . .

Then there was a click! Someone with
emergency brains had cut off something. And in
the dead silence that followed, I was able to begin
my lecture on "Recent Advances in Human Knowledge."

*   *   *   *   *

Such incidents unfortunately are few. Next
time I go on a lecture tour I'll carry my own
plumbers, and my own barbers, and my own
resurrection men, and have a good time all the
time.

*   *   *   *   *

But to return, one final moment, to my college
audiences. I found that college men—years out
of college—grave and dignified, heavy and tire-
some, are never tired of hearing again the old
yarns of their college days and losing weight and
dignity as they listen. . . . It is a solvent that

breaks up the heavy sediment the years have laid and shows again the bright surface of what once was.

All that reflects in a broad way what we call "the college spirit". You can't call it forth by giving it a lecture on "Recent Progress of Thermodynamics." What starts it into life is Memory—the vivifying picture that our imagination conjures up of the Days that Were! Always better and greater than the days that are—that wistful feeling towards the past that each of us carries within him—the call, back through the years, to a lost identity.

This college unity, college spirit, and with it the kindred link of the professions that spring from the college, is to my thinking the most binding tie that unites our otherwise divided country. In our economic life all is disunion—province against province and all against the Dominion, but we at least still have the bond of union represented by the common culture of our universities.

*   *   *   *   *

With that I leave *My Discovery of the West*.

FINIS.